How To Help Your Spouse
Heal From Your Affair

A Guide to Rebuilding Your Marriage

Table of Contents

Chapter 1: Introduction

'My wife doesn't understand that my hurt is real and my wounds are deep'. 'Just after acknowledging that he cheated he said he had been forgiven by God. It must be put behind us and let's get back together'.

There comes a moment when the unfaithful person comes clean about their affair and instantly feels relieved. They must have kept the relationship in the dark for weeks, months or even years. They may feel free of their shame or guilt. They don't have to stay in hiding anymore. The betrayed spouse, on the other hand, fear their worst nightmare has come true. Their world turns upside down. It is a very difficult place to be in and can crush you because you don't know how to navigate through this. The irrationality and unfairness of the situation can rip their heart out while the other person is experiencing relief. Let's begin with the unfaithful partner realizing that coming clean or being exposed doesn't end their duty towards their spouse. This is far from the truth. Ideally, you need to be present for your partner and everything you need to know is discussed in this book. The author invites you to get on the healing train for both people in the relationship.

It's important to be aware of the sufferings caused to people after finding out about betrayal in their relationship. They can turn insane. People who are in great suffering may reach a point where they experience a mental breakdown. Their nervous framework gives away and it pushes their mental capacity and they become ill in the face of dealing with the pain. They may even try to numb the pain or feelings. When pain is too difficult to deal with, people may tend to stay busy, start drinking or acting up in front of their close ones and try to suppress the condemnation, shame and the feeling of being inadequate. Another likely possibility is to turn bitter and resentful towards partner. This can end up in the couple being stuck. The betrayed may get frustrated that they are not getting the complete information and the unfaithful won't cooperate. It is tough to deal with bitterness because this induces a host of other emotions along with suffering and can really drive a person to do something they should not. It's inevitable. There is some level of bitterness that everyone will go through in this situation. Your lack of self-awareness can frustrate you. No one is perfect. No one will behave in a way that is particularity healing for both of them. But there is a difference between ending up stuck versus passing through the hallway of bitterness. The decision will have to come from you to not stay there. You will have to make a conscious decision to stay bitter and resent your spouse. It's going to have to be something that you decide to do. People choose to remain bitter. No one likes to be called to be accountable for their own emotions. Especially when they are victims of someone else's terrible immorality. Remember that it is life. You just need to pass through this stage, and something better awaits you. But if you stay there you will end up stuck and everyone who will encounter you will face your bitterness. Lastly, due to this great pain we are exposed to, we will love deeper and better. You will love in spite of all the challenges or circumstances you have faced. When everything goes to hell and you choose not to put a bed in the hallway and you move through it with steady progress even though slowly, you will arrive at a great place of deep gratitude, connection, and contentment in your life.

Today social media and our culture bring a mindset of showcasing perfection. People want to look perfect and make their partners look perfect and paint a rosy picture of their lives. It is all about what they are deriving. It is all self-centered and not about giving and sharing the truth and warmth but engaging in superficiality. A person's conditioning and their family environment while growing up plays a very important role in their present lives. Almost everyone comes from families where there are fights, secrecy, guilt or shame. There is no channel to communicate about anything such as your daily struggles, or boyfriends or girlfriends. So, your conditioning is such that you don't openly express how you feel, and you may get awkward when someone else expresses their feelings for you. Ask yourself if you were allowed to state your needs and expectations or were you focused on what others wanted from you. Evaluate if you were raised to be loyal towards people or were you raised to do what was right for you. Everyone generally advises you to do what you want and what makes you happy. This statement exists without consequences of how it will affect those who you love. You are a part of the large embedded community and you can't always pursue what you want without discerning the needs of others. One has to remember how they learned to love, did you learn from people who were protecting you or did you have to flee away for protection? Were you allowed to cry out loud or laugh out loud in your family? Were you touched, were you rocked or were you beaten or invaded or violated? What were the relationship boundaries like in your family? What was your place in the family? There is hardly anyone who can deny sexuality isn't central in any family. When you come out of your family, what do you look for? Whether it is comfort, protection, and love or is it the need for space and longing to escape or travel or wander around. These questions are deep-rooted in shaping your relationships. How you will react to being cheated or if you will ever cheat or not depends on the complexities of your past. All of us need security and adventures in our relationships. But one may need something more than the other. Your emotional history embodies the physicality of your sexuality.

Key embodiment of any relationship to speak its language one needs to ask, to take, to receive, to share, to refuse, to imagine and to give. It is about asking yourself just how comfortable you are asking for something or does it make you feel too dependent or does it make you subjugate? Or see if you feel people don't care about what you ask for because you are invisible to them and it may seem unimportant. Then you also need to evaluate if you are a giver. Do you enjoy giving? Do you feel the exuberance in your generosity? or do you acquit yourself to pay off your debts? Can you receive a compliment? and does it feel nice or do you start to qualify it? How vulnerable do you feel when you receive, and can you apply it sexually or do you only apply it interpersonally? Is it easy for you to share or do you find it massively scary and threatening? If you sit down to ask yourself about each of these actions and check your stance in each situation, you can get a pretty good portrait of yourself. You need to evaluate which one of the verbs need the most massaging and building around. Seek who is that one person who can hear you out and guide you through this process, who is the person who wants to give to you and you have been shutting them down and who is that person who you want to give and share something with. It goes from finding a map to identifying the core resource and strength that you need to muscle around and then actually act on it. Attachment in the life of a person can be secure or insecure or anxious. The ability to rely on someone who can share your distress, your joy and can respond to it appropriately without neglect, overemphasis on themselves, without pretending that it's for you when it is actually for them. A secure attachment is when we have a person who provides us with enough bandwidth to explore and are there for us and your relationship won't fall apart no matter what. If this is missing from a person's life, they may develop insecure attachments. It can be constant checking on the other person, going after them, picking fights to grab their attention and so on. You may become the pursuer in the relationship who always wants more or who needs to be assured or affirmed of the other person's intentions. You can also be a withholder who always withholds the conflict or closeness or afraid of being invaded. You may have learned to intentionally not come too close to save yourself from disappointment. Our attachments today are adaptive of the moment we were experiencing something bad earlier. It is adaptive and not a problem. It becomes a problem when you start doing this with someone who genuinely cares about you, loves you dearly and you are still responding to them from the place of your past where you learned it's better to stay distant to keep yourself safe. Usually, our strategies that we devised at the time to deal with a certain situation were useful then but may become redundant now.

Chapter 2: Relationships and Infidelity

A successful life is a melting pot of a lot of ingredients such as a good career, loving and caring people, healthy relationships and a good standard of living. In our lives, we can prioritize one over the other but can never completely ignore any. Each of these things makes an individual's world whole. The kind of relationships one keeps shapes their lives accordingly. A healthy, fulfilling and faithful relationship can help you face a bad day at work with a smile. When people are in love, everything seems possible. Problems get shared between you and your partner so that they don't seem like a big deal. A good relationship is central to every person's life. Every species that exist on our planet wants to keep itself safe. The front part of our brain controls impulses and helps us think critically and ensure our safety. Medulla helps to scan danger and be alert if situations demand so. There is another thing that human seeks to feel safe which is the human attachment. They attach themselves to feel secure and to share their emotions and thoughts. As babies, we need parents or caregivers to take care of us. As adults, we need someone to attach ourselves to. There are a few people who don't fathom any relationships and keep themselves detached. They don't like to commit and stay alone. That is a personal choice. The majority of people believe there is that one perfect person for them who will be the key they are looking for and will unlock all the doors of happiness and celebration in each other's lives.

Many find that perfect person in high school or at work or while riding a train or may still be searching. In today's technological world, people put their pride on the line in the name of online dating. Rejection can be so immediate and palpable, but you merely have to swipe right to find a date. To understand more about this new day and age love, there is no virtual risk. In case you swiped for a person and the other person doesn't swipe for you, they will never even know about you. Online dating provides a pool of choices and opportunities. Everyone is surrounded by potential mating alternatives and science says you are looking at them. About 50 years ago, researchers looked into why people persist to stay in relationships to understand the ultimate driving force in a relationship. Now, this brings a lot of factors to light. A prevalent theory at the time was John Thibaut and Harold Kelley's theory of interdependence. According to them, dependence is based on two processes. First is satisfaction. This measures how much your partner is meeting your most important needs. The second process is the quality of alternatives available around you. This means how desirable is your next best alternative to this relationship. A similar theory that can help to understand relationships is an investment scale. This is probably the most widely used scale today. This theory uses investment or resources that tie up the relationship which would get lost if the relationship ended. The higher the investment, the higher the loss. The more people are involved in a relationship at a given period the more damage control needs to be done once the relationship falls apart. An important observation here is that both theories evaluate the quality of an alternative available to an individual. Everyone puts value in finding the best match for them. We tend to devalue this evaluation when we are in a consciously satisfying and deeper relationship. But the minute the security begins to falter, we start to look for the next best alternative.

The whole dating and relationship scenario have seen a major shift. There is little or no stigma left around divorce. People accept failed relationships more than successful relationships. But the worst venom is infidelity. When infidelity strikes a relationship, it introduces the affected to a whole new world of pain. It is the worst feeling in the world. Infidelity happens to be the most prevalent reason for breaking off relationships and has increased multi fold in recent times. Your spouse or your partner, who has been your rock, the person who you shared several years with, had an affair. It smashes your whole apart. The people who surround you add to make it worse. It's heartbreaking to see your life getting discussed.

The situation is no better than a nightmare. After the initial shock of the situation comes to the anger. The anger is complimented with disgust and hatred. There is a breach of trust in your relationship. The situation affects not just the couple but everyone in their families.

Betrayal is a betrayal. When two people come together in a relationship, they share emotions and feelings that they don't share with anyone else. If one decides to go outside the relationship and seek comfort and share their life with someone else, this is infidelity. This breach can be sexual or emotional. Sexual intimacy with someone other than your partner is painful. It hits you hard. It can be perceived with just sex or just a physical act. The offender may try to convince the betrayed by calling it a one-time mistake. The other type of infidelity is emotional. For a long period, this wasn't even considered a form of betrayal. To be emotionally intimate with someone other than your partner can be easily denied. It can be perceived as a close friendship. It can or can't be sexual but being sexually intimate here is not the key. The important fact is to trust someone enough to share your feelings and your life with other than your partner. The connection here is much stronger. The emotions involved are much more complex. Usually, the offender is just at the brink of breaking into a sexual relationship with this other person and has not been involved in it yet. But the emotions and feelings are all there. The offender can easily argue the relationship to be a close friendship and confuse the betrayed by calling their feelings irrational. Whether there is an actual breach of trust or emotions is still not known to the betrayed. Where the betrayed suffers internally by not being able to express the doubt and the offender denying their mistake, the relationship falters and falls apart. It won't be wrong to say that this kind of intimacy is much harder to recover from than a sexual relationship.

There is adultery in any relationship when the people involved don't share or feel love for each other. Even if no other person is involved the original relationship has no footing. Betrayal is very individualistic. It can differ from situation to situation. What can be perceived as infidelity by one may not be a betrayal for the other. The responses and reactions of the people around us impact everything that happens in our lives from that point on. It is statistically true that about 60% of people have suicidal thoughts after infidelity. The result is not good. With the relationship put in a maze, the betrayed loses the ability to trust their partner or anyone else. The feeling sucks you into a period of depression. The person is filled with self-doubt, loses confidence in terms of judging someone's character. There is a constant feeling of rage and hurt combined that takes a long time to heal or recover. The feeling of being betrayed again depends on the person who is suffering from it. In a fresh relationship, if the partner cheats, it can be easier to let go. 'There is plenty of fish in the sea', 'She didn't deserve you'. These are some common responses and it is definitely hurtful but can be learned from and people can move on. If someone is in a longer- term relationship, the hurt it causes to the betrayed can vary leaps and bounds. This is when someone's nature will dictate how much they get plunged into darkness. Some people complain of not being able to remove the pictures mentally. Some suffer from sleepless nights. Some may get depressed. The kind of feelings that may hit the affected can't be easily understood. No amount of reading human psychology can prepare you to face these circumstances.

It is difficult to control the anxiety. The pressing need to check your partner's mobile phones, endless fights with the partner, feeling of self-doubt and trying to find an escape to the situation or trying to reason with the behavior of your offending partner. These complex emotions can't be enunciated enough. This can be termed as relationship trauma and is very similar to Post Traumatic Stress Disorder. The parts of a day or people that you would have enjoyed, like going to the park, visiting your friends or family become difficult to comprehend since it's hard to face anyone. Besides this the feeling of what's wrong with me, why did this happen to me are even more heart quenching. The actual focus should be on what went wrong. The relationship between these two people has sometimes nothing to do with cheating. The relationship can be perfectly fine and still people go outside to seek comfort. It is much easier to say that the offender cheated because they shared a bad relationship. These days, with easy divorces, if people have poor relationships, they seek divorce. However, if they go outside marriage, it usually means they don't want to lose their original partner. There are some things they don't want to let go and hold on to but still go out of the marriage to seek something that is missing. This complexity is usually ignored since it is difficult to describe and explain. No theory of infidelity can explain the absolute nature of it in terms of how it affects the relationships. Infidelity in different ages has managed to top a relationship no matter how much a relationship may adapt or develop.

We try to realize the reason why people try to break free from a relationship and risk to hurt someone who they have vowed to be together with. These vows have been created by the two people with their own will. The vows to stay together, have children, have a perfect house and intended job.

What changes and triggers someone to break free from the shackles is the fault of no one but the person themselves. It's not you. You feel shattered and gutted because socially and personally it breaks everything down. It's amazing how one day we wish for certain things and the next day we may want to be completely detached from it and perceive them as something that is imprisoning us. How a person who is completely sexually shut down with their original partner is lustful and eager and how they can't bring it home. Matrimony started by being an imposition on women to mark exclusiveness. This has now changed to dual-gender commitment. To put it simply, instead of giving more freedom to women, we have taken away freedom from men. Ideally, we need to embrace the complexity of relationships and what infidelity of the relationship is feasting on rather than being superficial and saying the easy thing to say and doing the easy thing to do. It is wrong to define infidelity in an ambit of extremity and describing that as the norm and ultimately measuring every circumstance in that light. There is a difference between trying to understand and trying to justify. It is necessary to understand the circumstance and then act rather than passing judgments, being narrow-minded and engaging in discrimination against the offending partner because this won't help partners, families and their children.

Chapter 3: Society today is fertile ground for traitors

The world has completely changed today compared to even the past decade. Social media platforms and applications like Tinder, Bumble and so on have made communication very easy. With easy communication, there is a pathway to easy connections. These connections develop into relationships and since these relationships have lower tangibility, they may not last long. Although it is not a conclusive statement this is what is generally noticed by experts. Again, the whole scenario of online dating is not to be blamed for this. It is also a matter of personal choice. For relationships that begin online, about 17% end up getting married. There have always been rules in a marriage or a relationship. What is perceived as friendship and what is crossing the line has to be mutually agreed on and clear. But these rules have experienced a major shift in the past decade. From the dialed up internet age to the fastest network accessed by almost everyone, the dating game has also had an upgrade. There are over 360 million people who have their accounts on Facebook, 69 million on Twitter, over one billion people on Instagram and so on in the year 2019. All it takes is to Google the name of a person you wish to connect with and with a little information, you can access their pictures and a large portion of their lives. With this information, it is relatively easier to strike a conversation, think and carefully craft the conversation, make an impression and a build relationship. If a person has met their partner online and isn't satisfied with the relationship, a person may think of finding another partner online. Even if you start a conversation with someone without any preconceived notion of cheating on your partner, it can develop into something more than friendship without you realizing it. In your head, you may have conceived the idea that it is possible to have a relationship with this person someday in the future. It is possible to fall in love with someone's words and get really intimate really fast. This serves our right and our need for belonging and intimacy. The opportunities that were not available before are easily available now. A section of society exists that exercises gender dominance and finds it appropriate to cheat while staying married to their partners. It is a shame that people hide behind the covers of culture and religion and find it appropriate to get involved with more than one person. The problem here is not just one sex being allowed to have more partners, it's the forbid dance of the contrary. This narcissism definitely stems from cultural dominance and precedents in the families that raise them. Infidelity is considered morally acceptable in various parts of the world.

The quality of our lives is defined by the success or failure we see in our relationships. No one on their death beds wishes for an extra day of work. Our lives revolve around the love we get from our parents growing up and our friends and ultimately our partners. If we talk about relationships in general, not much change has been noticed in a relationship of a baby with his caregivers or of siblings or your relationship with your doctor. The relationship that has seen an exorbitant change in recent times is a couple. Sexuality which was earlier rooted in procreation is now replaced with desire, lust, and connection. A couple together provides each other with economic, social support, children, a good standard of living and so on. In addition to being one another's best friend, confidant, intellectually equal, a passionate lover, inspiration and the list goes on. It takes lesser requirements to start a business than the number of pressure couples today feel. Everyone seeks a lot more than what they used to, and this is before technology entered your bedrooms. A couple has had so many experiences, it's so complex to analyze a couple and disintegrate every problem because of the complexity of the circumstances involved. There is no school for a relationship. A lot of people feel doubtful at various stages in a relationship with no one to guide them and all this happens because there is no one who they can turn to for advice. Imagine the pressure when people determine love in their twenties and wish for it to stay for the next fifty years with unconditional love and passion and commitment. Where the format of a swiping culture is great, it brings a lot of choices to people, but it also brings the anxiety of how to know the person is the one when there are hundreds of other matches that you haven't contacted yet. There is a major lack of face to face communication to build serious relationships. With the introduction of television, mobile phones, laptops, and more and more devices, our time is taken by technology rather than building personal connections. Major concerns of people's lives are rather discussed over texts and then people complain about misunderstandings. When people wish for a relationship which has everything they dream of, they should also inculcate the resilience it takes to make it work. The ups and downs, the fights and vacations and betrayals, it is imperative to grow for a couple to withstand the challenges it brings. And this spirit is exactly what is missing.

The majority of people struggle in naming one perfect, ideal relationship they look up to. You can immediately name your favorite businessman, favorite athlete or favorite musician. If you want to make a business successful, you need to fall in love with your customer, perceive everything from their eyes, and deliver quality every single time. Similarly, for anyone who wants to have an intimate relationship, there are no perfect models to learn from. So, let's start by discussing what goes wrong in a relationship. When there is a paradigm shift from what you are giving to what you are getting in the relationship, the problems start to arise. In couple's therapy, no one comes to look into their lives, they come to fix their partners. People don't want to change themselves. The notion that 'you are responsible for my happiness and because of you, I am miserable' is what needs a turnaround. This notion makes you angry and resentful and with the increasing emotions, you as a couple are drifting apart. The distance then brings other people in the picture who will understand you better than your partner and cause infidelity. There is a plethora of options to choose from. It is so simple to put a password on the phone and change it now and then, meet new people online and form connections or delete a conversation on the phone. This makes cheating easy and so some people jump in to get a piece of the action. People who cheat may have ruined some lives but can move ahead to make other relationships faster today and this is where the biggest setback of online dating lies. People constantly lie on the internet. A lot of people lie about their ages, preferences, height, weight or any other personal details and it's so easy to fall into the trap. This can be extremely dangerous too. The internet does provide an easy arena to cheat.

People who have their accounts on social media are already a part of online love. If a man leaves his sleeping wife and goes to have sex with another woman, it is cheating. Some may agree if he sits on his couch and talks to the other woman about his thoughts and emotions, it is also cheating. If a man appreciates a woman's social media account and spends a lot of time checking her out, is that also cheating? There are a lot of questions that need to be navigated through in a relationship today. There is no set questionnaire that you can fill out to know everything you need to know about your partner.

Everything cannot be easily articulated. Some things are felt and not said. But these factors impact every relationship today. Imagine how well relationships can work if one is open about every infatuation, every feeling and every emotion that erupts in their mind and the partner understands them and stays by their side. Fantasizing while having sex, oral sex, attempting to seduce, sending flirty messages constitute cheating. Society today plays a major influence on people's mind. People may have a cheating gene in them since forever but may have not been able to tap into it and act upon it due to lack of opportunity. If you put them in today's dating scene, they may find it easy to cheat on people. Ultimately the paradox of blame lies on both society and the traitor. It is not fair to hold one responsible singularly.

Chapter 4: Betrayal has no gender and age

All people are different. When moving from adolescence to adulthood, society imbibes various postulations into the mind of an individual. There are so many cultural influences, religious beliefs and individualistic behavior that shapes a person's life. Society, in general, is plagued by failed marriages, divorces, unhealthy and abusive relationships. Every age brings its new challenges. In the teen years, a person attempts to get aligned with their sexuality while struggling with inner insecurities and external influences. This is a sensitive age and relationships at this age can afford to be more experimental. Precarious bonds or bad experiences can impact and shape future relationships. Immaturity and jealousy are inevitable. It is a phase of exploring newer things and trying to break free. Being young and being free is a wondrous feeling and fills your heart with excitement. When parents try to monitor the behavior, it is perceived as bondage. Accepting the advice and acting on it seems to be the last thing they want to do. The tendency to break free develops and the same gets reflected onto the relationship. The urge to be free, careless, independent and wild clouds the mind and they may seek the same in other relationships. Tying up with one single person while imagining there are a lot of options in the world seems exciting. They search for freedom in friendships and relationships which may dwindle if they are tied down. However, having multiple relationships also clears up what a person wants in their lives but without hurting anyone's feelings.

A young adult who is just coiled in a relationship and wishes to build a family unit faces various emotions. To build a relationship, various hurdles need to be passed. Acceptance of the partner, managing finances and getting along with each other's families are to name a few. The innate need to break free from these shackles of responsibilities and enduring commitment can push a person or bring him to the edge of looking for an escape.

Every human being has a flair for freedom. Some can fight it, and some cannot. Therefore, cheating is a matter of personal choice devoid of age or gender. While struggling with managing a new life if there is someone who promises comfort and an out from the routine then one is drawn to that. Those who refrain from settling down are in the fear of growing up. These people refuse to commit and get into long term relationships and maybe likely to jump from one relationship to another just because they don't want to be tied down.

Around the middle years, an adult who is in a relationship that has sustained several years, comes to follow a routine. Routine by definition is a series of actions that are being followed repeatedly. Everyone despises getting into a rut and many fall into it without realizing. It is one of the most feared scenarios in a relationship. The matter of losing something despite having everything is inexplicable and the person starts questioning the relationship to the point that he yearns to look out of the relationship. The charm and passion that seems to have lost its luster in this old relationship and seek to flow out through this other person. The betrayal at this stage is hurtful because of so many invested years. The man turns to younger women to experience the newness that they lack. It's equivalent to reliving their youth. On the other hand, the woman who is almost entering the menopausal phase of her life and questioning her womanhood and feeling unexpressed chases after someone else to get in touch with her sexuality and to feel desired again. She craves for attention more than ever and if the opportunity arises, she might go for it.

It is believed that men cheat more than women. But women have come to be equals in this race and tend to cheat just as much as men. Men cheat due to falling into a routine. They may feel unsatisfied or under-appreciated. They may find an opportunity to cheat with few chances of getting caught. For example, it is only a one-time thing. They may get addicted to pornography. There is no breathing space in the relationship. Women may cheat due to insecurities such as approaching an older age or changing bodies. Women are usually more accommodating and are more suppressed under family and social pressures than men. She may get too saturated with the impositions and look to break free. She may feel she doesn't get the attention or care she deserves from her partner. The other person is not sensitive to her sexual needs. In some cases, she may just be bored. For men, it's more of an egoistic matter of getting the woman to like them. For women, it may be a perfect way to get their emotional pangs satisfied.

Statistically, around 53% of people who cheat on their spouses are married. Only 6% of cheaters confess to cheating on their spouses. Men tend to leave women more often by 22%, when they find out about their cheating. About 35% of women live in denial of their men cheating and refuse to act on it. Women can cheat better than men because they are better liars. 8% to 15% of children haven't been fathered by the person who feels he is the biological father. Both men and women are likely to cheat.

There is a huge communication gap between the couple. Communication is key in any relationship. Differences arise when one doesn't speak their heart out and reserves inhibitions in their minds to protect their feelings. This leads to accumulating emotions that burst out and cause serious fights. The accumulation of problems is worse than solving individual and isolated battles. The gap doesn't widen and understanding, and compatibility grow with time. However, reserving doubts in the mind and bearing questionable or unsatisfactory behavior of your partner just pushes you to get exhausted from the relationship.

The partner is unable to provide for your financial needs. Most people are unapologetic ally materialistic, and they must have their requirements fulfilled. They yearn for maintaining a standard of living and derive pleasure in spending money. Women are accused of being gold diggers, however men can be just the same. There are as many dependent men as are women. Educational loans, childcare loans, and business loans impact the stress levels of a person and a pressuring spouse is the last thing they can handle. Before entering in the relationship, financial matters must be necessarily discussed and either one should be able to provide for the other's needs or they must be equals with no burden on a single person to fulfill every whim of the other person.

Constant fights and misunderstandings can pressure anyone to leave their present state and look for better avenues. With the number of opportunities available for people, no one likes to stay unhappy. Everyone itches to move forward in life and if the people in the relationship refuse to reflect on the reason of the misunderstanding and let the gap grow, the other person who simply agrees with them more will tempt them to fall out of love. Fights help people to make their relationship stronger. When the fights are recurring and they aren't resolved properly, you can anticipate that one might set their heart on someone else who isn't so complicated to deal with.

Abuse, whether it is emotional or physical, makes a person fall out of love. Abusive relationships bring the victim a world of pain. Emotional abuse happens when one person manipulates, controls and isolates their partner and makes them helpless. Their growth is almost stinted, and their anxiety and stress levels are high, devoid of being around the other person or not. Physical abuse is literal in the sense of hurting the person by slapping or beating. A person can turn abusive due to plenty of reasons such as having a bad reputation at work, low self-esteem, and general hatred and so on. The other person must prepare an exit plan immediately in such situations. Physical abuse puts a person off almost immediately. Such a relationship preludes its end, but a relationship infected by emotional abuse may take some time to get out of. The person may find solace in someone else who appears to be their well-wisher or an old friend who is familiar and consoling. The higher the period of misbehavior, the higher are the chances of cheating.

Betrayal hits hard and leaves a wreck behind which makes it extremely difficult to get past. It leaves the victim shook and their soul stained. The one who is cheated on gets filled with self-doubt. The fear of what they failed to provide to the person that they were drawn to cheat is ever daunting. This is followed by an extreme amount of anger which surfaces due to unfairness of the situation. The fear of the unknown and unstable future, at that moment, clouds the brain. One needs to think about rebuilding one's life again. In some situations, it can be harder than anything else. In longer relationships, codependency happens to be natural and it is very hard to get over. The ironic feeling of not being able to live with the person and the hatred to see their face confuses, irritates and disturbs you.

At different ages, betrayal is dealt with differently. In the adolescent years, the victim behaves the most violently and recklessly to the situation. Due to a lack of maturity, the affected may turn suicidal or clinically depressed. The manner to deal with the situation doesn't come naturally to them so like every other emotion, reaction to this situation is heightened and they may act up. As a young adult faced by betrayal, it fills the person with suspicion about themselves. The whole vacillates and the foundation of every new relationship is affected by this failed one. If a person is cheated on in their middle age, they try to dust it under the carpet after sustaining the initial shock. They both try to come to an agreement to stay together or end up in a divorce in a mature manner. Usually, the couple has children and they are the priority for every parent. The focus shifts towards them and their well-being is always a concern.

Chapter 5: Warning signs of a betrayal

Trust your intuitions. The majority of cases of infidelity hide in the dark because the offender is never caught. Perhaps, the person is very careful or the one who is cheated on is blinded by the love of the unfaithful and fails to see the deed. However, there will be some oddities in the behavior of the unfaithful and you need to see them. These behavioral changes should not go unnoticed and attention and alertness are imperative. Ignoring the signs and staying in denial will end up in hurting the soul more than facing it. The lies and wrong deeds just accumulate to the point they become hard to ignore and there is little to no hope left for the relationship to survive. You must look for these silent signs without tipping them off. There are plenty of ways to know if your partner is cheating on you or not, but you must not lose context. In singularity, some oddities don't mean your spouse is sleeping with someone else or is connected to someone else emotionally. You must look at the bigger picture and look for changes in the patterns of behavior. Be patient to understand the reason for something out of the norm.

Your partner is suddenly very possessive about their mobile phones or laptop or any electronic device and refuses to let you touch them. You should be concerned when they are being more secretive about this than before. It clearly points towards their aversion to you finding out about who they are communicating with. In times of technological indulgence when it is not hard to maintain proximity with anyone, mobile phones play a significant role in increasing a connection or maintaining one. They have changed their computer passwords and shut down their computer when you are around them while they are working. Be aware if you notice late-night phone calls and them becoming secretive about the caller. This shouldn't feel deemed to keep a check on your spouse's phone obsessively for signs of a potential third party. If the person has somehow become compulsive about the whereabouts of their phone or is getting calls that they refuse to take in front of you, this can be a matter of concern.

Your spouse is changing their dressing style or is concerned about their looks more than usual. Perhaps they are spending extra time in the gym to get in shape or taking extra time to get ready in the morning or dressing impressively on what appears to be casual outings. This is in no way definitive of a person who is looking for someone to chat with but if these occurrences shoot in your mundane routines, this may be a trigger. If you find yourself in this situation, it's advisable to be alert and watch your partner's activities closely and attempt to have open conversations about your concerns.

They are losing interest in going out with you or watching a Netflix series which was your favorite activity to do together. More than usual they are getting out of plans you had agreed on earlier. They are using excuses to not meet you or ignoring your calls incessantly for no real fault of your own. You must give them the benefit of the doubt in this situation, however, if it is repetitive and it seems as if they are blowing you off, there is a possibility of a third person in the relationship.

Your partner has stopped wearing an engagement ring or may take it off more often. This is a passive sign which you shouldn't concern yourself with a lot. However, if it is happening in addition to other odd changes then you can be more skeptical. Keep an eye out on for the pattern of them not wearing the ring- whether they have casually opted out of wearing it or do they remove it when they go out with their friends or at work? If your friends also feel any changes in your relationship and they show concerns about your behavior with each other, it can be a sign. Pay heed to what they are pointing at.

There may be a vivid change in their behavior or habits such as you may observe a new way of talking or use of certain words that they never used before. They may start listening to a different type of music. Unlike before, they are coming back home later and their breath smells of alcohol or they may smell of an unfamiliar scent. They may turn to take a shower immediately after returning from work unless they work at a construction site or work of such nature. These are not evident indicators of your partner having an affinity towards someone else. But a person of routine may raise red flags if there is a sudden change in their behavior or habits. They may have suddenly shown an interest in joining a beginner's class or may pursue some activity or hobby which they haven't been interested in before. You may hear them change their stance about politics or any other matter about which they were rigid in the past. They may start talking about movies, series or anything entertaining that is unlike their taste. A person can usually pick up some hobby and there is nothing peculiar about it. However, if it seems inappropriate or odd to their being and they aren't able to justify the reasons properly, there may be a chance of someone else involved. People in long term relationships tend to be aware of routine affairs and any such activity can ring cheating bells in your mind. Be patient before jumping to conclusions.

There are unexplained expenses on your spouse's account, or they may ask you to open separate bank accounts. There can be various variations to this. Be on the lookout for unusual bank transactions. Observe if they are visiting the ATM too often and don't hold back if you have doubts or their activities seem sneaky. You may find them buying new clothes or making other extravagant expenses. Look for any hotel bookings or recurring deposits to an unknown account. Don't ignore if you see new and expensive things that they own and can't explain the nature or the source of them. Illicit financial transactions are a portent of something sneaky happening in a relationship and can be very tricky to deal with. It is best to deal with such situations and giving them much bandwidth to either give the benefit of the doubt or to conceal the truth and investigate without tipping off the other person.

They may start talking about friends they have never had before, or you may have never heard of and they suddenly start hanging out with someone you aren't comfortable around. This may simply be a way of getting some time away from you. They may take unexplained trips for the sake of business or with friends and don't seem keen to share exact details with you. They may start working late and even go to work on weekends. They may refuse to meet friends who have high moral grounds.

They start blaming you for everything wrong in your relationship. They refuse to assume responsibility for anything. They seem to forget things they said previously or just tend to get forgetful about things. A major sign is if they don't want to engage with you sexually. Try to figure out the reason for sex deterioration in the relationship or lookout for any changes in their sex habits. This can be a sign or the reason why the relationship is faltering. If the couple is not open about their sexual needs to one another or one doesn't deliver, they may easily fall out of love and look for better suited. Neither men nor women hold back in seeking what they wish out of a person. Sex deterioration is a part of every marriage. After a couple has kids or is coiling in the complexities of life, it is not easy to keep the same level of prowess in the bed. But the couple can drift apart and there is no love felt or left, the other person can be drawn to someone else who is ready to provide them with everything missing in their life. It won't be wrong to say you, or your partner are a closed book about your sexuality, differences will grow, and the relationship will be more likely to fail.

There is a difference in the way they meet you than before. They don't look in your eyes while talking to you and don't kiss you before they leave for work or do any other routine habits they used to do. They may stop giving you compliments. They may accuse you of invading their personal space and guilt you into believing they aren't doing anything wrong. They take more care about their appearance devoid of constant fights and lack of affection from each other. On the contrary, your spouse may become very attentive towards you or may make uncommon gestures. This may be flattering but make sure this is not overcompensation or a cover-up for something wrong.

They may start shrugging responsibilities such as distancing themselves from their children or other family members. They may refuse to pick your children from school or accompanying them to classes, not attend their school meetings or refrain from spending extra time with them. Your child may start to feel ignored and unloved. Along with being irresponsible, you may notice a shift in their attitude towards spiritual matters. They may start to defend people who cheat. They may avoid attending church services or behave differently in front of a morally correct individual who can be a friend or a family member.

If your goal is to have a successful and healthy connection, you should be able to trust your partner for letting them into your heart. Some specific signs for men cheating are you surely know your partner inside out. You know how he reacts when he is happy, angry, stressed, tired or bored. However, one of the most prominent characteristics of a man who is cheating is when he acts out of character. Their typical behavior, routine, and actions begin to change. For example, the amount of time he is spending in the bathroom has increased. There may be subtle changes. Earlier he would watch the football match in the drawing-room and now he watches them locked in his room. These nuances tend to be wake up calls and need more attention.

Ask yourself if something is wrong if your man suddenly starts to worry about his looks when he couldn't care less about it before. If he starts to buy expensive clothes, wears high end cologne or starts working out or gets too keen to be in shape, when such thoughts haven't even passed his mind in the past. When a man becomes suddenly obsessed with his looks, this shift in his personality can show that he is playing the field.

It is a fact that over 66 % of men are guilty of cheating. So, he may try to assuage you and catch you in praise and flattery. Another powerful indicator of your man cheating is if he pulls away all of a sudden. When men cheat, they put all their attention and focus elsewhere. They become less interested and invested in your well-being and events in your life as a couple. If he is acting distant all of a sudden, it's not a far-off possibility that he is cheating on you.

If he has been a cheater in the past, he is likely to be a cheater. There are two kinds of cheaters. The first type is the people who feel extremely bad about cheating and the second type is the narcissistic kind of cheater. If your man belongs to the second type, don't be surprised if he cheats on you. It's in his nature to cheat and he can't stay loyal to you. The first type is circumstantial. It has been found that even when some men are in fulfilling relationships, they still have a proclivity to cheat. So, if your fulfilling and intimate time together with a couple has reduced significantly or it seems all rushed, distracted and uninterested, he may be sowing his wild oats somewhere else.

He may be quintessentially lying to you. It is a common characteristic of a cheating man. He may lie about where he is, with whom he is, where he is spending his money on or who he is calling or texting. Liars tend to repeat what they are saying as if it is rehearsed or give a lot of unnecessary details while talking. They seem to touch or cover their mouth, fidget or shake nervously signaling that they are probably holding something back.

Another major indicator of cheating men is they say the wrong name. It's not uncommon that the name of the person who he is cheating with ends up popping out of his mouth, sometimes even at inappropriate times. He may suddenly have a new need for privacy. This is because when he cheats it is an important part of keeping the illusion of his innocence. Keep an eye on his company. The quality of his friends and colleagues influence him the most. Usually, a person who cheats typically hangs out with other men who cheat. Over 80% of cheating men are friends with someone who cheats too.

A definite sign that a woman is cheating that you should not ignore is when she starts talking about someone who she works with or some friend more than usual. At that point, she might not be cheating on you with that guy, but she is thinking about him. This may or may not develop into a deep connection. If she doesn't show any interest in your problems or winnings, she is most likely to be cheating. This is because women are naturally caring so if she acts absolved of all sensitivity towards you, she is not that into you anymore. She might go missing for a long time. Being aware of her usual whereabouts, if she makes a plan to meet people you have never heard of or she is unable to explain who she spent time with, she is likely to be cheating on you.

She may start working later than her normal hours. This should raise suspicion if you know she is not that into her work. If she starts assuming the time you will meet her or obsessively asks about the time when you will be back home, it is surely a sign. She accuses you of cheating. This is called formatting reaction. The motive is to divulge the blame on the other person because of guilt or regret.

Chapter 6: How to face a betrayal

Being betrayed is one of the worst nightmares for anyone. The consequences can be devastating. The whole belief system shakes at first glance. Various emotions surface and involuntary thoughts begin to haunt your mind. It is a question that pervades the betrayed "but why". Often it happens to be preceded by suspicions. Even if one happens to be aware and prepared to face the devil, the trauma is always very strong. It hits like a hurricane when you see the person you invested in agreeing to the fact that they cheated you. You have a mixture of highly explosive feelings, you continually think, leaving a deep wound in your soul. Try not to be overwhelmed by post-traumatic stress. One loses their sleep, finds it difficult to concentrate, loses weight and can be pushed to the extreme such as depression or life-ending thoughts. No one likes to face or talk about their partner cheating on them. In an ideal world, not a single person would like to deal with the heartbreak that comes after being cheated on. However, it is a harsh reality. Open and honest conversations must precede the need for seeking out an extramarital affair.

When we pick a person and attach ourselves with them, they may choose to stay in unhealthy relationships even where there are problems. If there is a secretive behavior on part of the partner, the person who is cheated on suffers from attachment distress on a very primal level. The moment the person is aware of the betrayal, the distress is profound. Some people fall on to their knees, cry for hours and think about why they even care and why is it so dramatic for them, when they hear about the betrayal for the first time. The initial reaction can also take a route of running away from the shock and shutting yourself down. This whittles away from overbearing unfaithful who is belittling the problem and calling it a misunderstanding or plain overreaction from their end. As an unfaithful person, the reveal can end up with them dealing with either a fight, freeze or flight from their partner. Both unfaithful and the betrayed experience grief, confusion, and gush of emotions that need to be dealt with. The more attached the couple is, the more is the extent of grief. It is riveting to feel that after being betrayed they are exposed to the world. Denial, anger, bargaining, moments of acceptance are cycling in the mind of the betrayed. Bargaining refers to oscillating thoughts of 'what-ifs'. If I lose weight and get attractive, maybe he will come back. If we go for counseling, everything will be okay. The unfaithful may go through the feeling of loss as well. On experiencing their partners acting out, they may immediately think that the relationship is all over and is irretrievable.

When the unfaithful experiences their partner leaning into the situation after finding out the truth, they may find out the betrayed has become highly vigilant. They begin to question everything and yearn for safety. They may become reactive to perceived abandonment. They will be hypersensitive about any further conversation with their cheating partner. They might stick to little nuances and feel more abandoned and distressed.

When faced with more information, it may crush them, or it may even make them act up or not react at all in a span of ten to twenty minutes. The response to every minute detail can be extreme or a piece of huge information can derive no reaction out of the sufferer. At this moment the unfaithful, having caused a lot of atrocity to the betrayed, should feel the need to be available for the other person's acting out, distress and unpredictability. They need to be valiant to make them feel safe in those moments of primal panic. It is important to bear in mind that at the moment, the person is experiencing a break-in safety. It is irrelevant if it is real or perceived. There is no need to preach to them about what is real and what is perceived. It is a biological response and can't be treated with rationalizing at least at that very second. Your next thought must be how you can help them. Do your best to not get defensive. Own up to your mistakes. This is very hard to do since the other person may be fighting and our natural response to a fight is defense. Try to just care for them. There should be a questioning process between the aching partner and the unfaithful to understand their feelings better. The thought of making an effort to maximize their comfort should be a priority. Just be there, sit with them and assist them in their pain.

Another response at that moment can be running away after encountering the situation. It may be physical disappearance or emotional leaving where the person completely shuts down in front of you. Immediately the hurt may think off hurting and betraying the unfaithful. This spur of giving it back to their cheating spouse is almost involuntary. The unfaithful may jump to conclude that their relationship has come to an end. They may perceive it as the ultimate sign that their partner is going to flee and is easily going to move on whereas this can just be a mechanism of coping with the trauma by the hurt. It is safety seeking behavior. They are just dealing with the distress of dealing with the situation. The pendulum of emotions where they want to get intimate one day and the next day they want to end the relationship and take their kids away from the betraying partner, these are all reactions caused through the adrenaline rush at the different courses of time.

Shifting focus on what the betrayed can do after encountering a cheating partner, will let your emotions cloud you. It is completely natural to be confused. However, bring yourself out of the numbness and experience these feelings. Don't subdue anything you feel. Allowing an emotional build-up will not benefit you in any way. Journalize or write up about what you are experiencing. Take some time out. Enter your own space. Try to seclude anything that reminds you of the person. If you are living together, it will be best to move out for some time. If you are in a long- term relationship, don't talk to the unfaithful. You may want to steer clear of social media. Try to avoid stalking them or going through your pictures together and just try to keep your mind off it. Refrain from doing something extreme. Getting a makeover or joining the gym to get in shape is normal. Try not to bad mouth your partner, create a scene in the family, and file for divorce as an initial reaction. This impulse may lead you to regret later. This shall not be confused to be an insinuation towards acceptance or forgiveness. These matters should be well thought of for ensuring the safety of the betrayed more than the cheating partner. There is no such thing as absolute revenge. Revenge may just temporarily heal you. It causes more harm than good. The real revenge is soaking the situation in and making the other person repent on their own. There is no better satisfaction than the satisfaction of being in the right.

Seek professional help to deal with the pain. It is impossible to get over the pain and distress caused by your loved one in a day. You can rely on a friend or your parents or if you don't feel comfortable to have your life discussed, visit a psychiatrist. Speak your heart out and start your healing process. Think about getting better. Try to avoid negative thoughts and most importantly steer clear of anything that reminds you about them. It is hard to do but it is necessary. Cry it out, act on it, indulge in going out with your friends, staying out for late hours, party hard, plan a vacation, and buy something you wished to but were holding back. The whole point is to make sure you heal your soul and spirit with the least damage done to your well-being. Don't correspond with their family members or any of their close friends. Take enough time before you are ready to meet the person again. Confront them bravely. Be strong headed when you meet them and don't go back into the maze of feeling lost and uncertainty. Reflect on what went wrong. At this point when you have had time to heal, dig up the reason for ending up in this situation. Think about your future. Worry about your kids. It may even involve you getting on your feet again. Don't look for someone else immediately. It is acceptable to sulk and to make people around you feel your pain. It's more about having an outlet of your feelings. But once you are past that, jump on to move ahead in life. You can get in touch with someone who is suffering from a similar heartbreak. You must try to find an opportunity at such times to improve and grow past the situation.

If it is too had to come in terms with the situation, rather than moving towards something devastating, try to understand what made the relationship fall out. Unless you were in a dead-end relationship with a person who is patterned to be a cheater, that one is on you. The focal point should be rewinding and looking for signs and causes that you think led to the betrayal. It is seldom a one-way stream. Both people in a relationship have failed to fulfill some need of the other person. Be hopeful that the relationship can be saved which seems distant right now. In the chaos, don't ignore the behavior of your partner at this time. The hard part of facing your partner and having a conversation with them is ineludible. You need to hold conversations to talk with an initial pace of conversation with your partner to know if they intend to save the marriage. Where do you both stand after facing the blow of infidelity? Are you both keen on breaking the relationship? If not, then what's holding you back? What specifics of the affair do you need to know about? Why did your partner need this other person? Where did they meet them? Before venturing into the physicality of their illicit relationship, you may need to consult a psychiatrist or a trusted friend or your family beforehand. Now take time to evaluate and reach a certain point of view. See if they are sorry, remorseful or disinterested. Talk about your conversation with your partner with someone you trust.

Sometimes the betrayed experiences a rage due to a pressing need to talk about the extent the unfaithful partner went to and they refuse to provide details or may not care to make amends. If you wonder why they divulge from providing you the details you want them to reveal, don't take this the hard way and don't indulge in self-doubt. For the unfaithful to withhold the information is the most selfish thing that they can do at this moment. It's enough that they have ripped their partner's heart out and yet refuse to provide them with what they deserve to know. To not provide them the information is similar to leaving someone to solve a jigsaw puzzle in darkness. The cheating partner is most likely to be too ashamed or the details are too painful to discuss, and they might feel you won't be able to handle it. When the betrayed person tries to put all the pieces together, they aren't trying to shame you. They are just trying to put all the pieces together. An unfaithful person doesn't particularly enjoy talking about his affair, addiction, choices and pain because it is uncomfortable. However, the betrayed spouse cannot heal without being able to talk about what has happened. If they don't get this information, they may get infuriated. Their imagination can go wild and they may start to imagine what happened and what did not happen. They try to put together different scenes and imagine the worst and ultimately their pain compounds. They are unaware about what to forgive. They remain in the state of paralysis. Most probably the unfaithful can't talk about it because they are not healed. When shame is triggered, people usually shut down and it may seem impossible for them to bring their disloyalty out in the open. The unfaithful may fear to relive their mistakes more than the betrayed wanting to hear the information, hence the silence.

Another reason why they must be holding back is probably because there may be more to the story that what they previously admitted to. They feel they will lose a chance of any kind of restoration if they reveal all the missing pieces. To avoid the situation, the betrayed must ensure them that they will digest all the information and wait before jumping to any conclusions. This may be stoically agonizing to do but if you want to have full disclosure, this is something that you must agree to do.

Chapter 7: Consequences of a betrayal on children

It is in no way questionable that in a failing relationship, the biggest impact falls on the children. Children love their parents and in every household, parents are their role models. Comparatively, children these days are closer to their parents while growing up than kids who were born in the 1980s or 1990s. Parents should assume responsibility in looking after their children by keeping their personal battles aside since any fall out in their upbringing can change their lives for worse. It is really important to see a failed relationship from the eyes of adolescents and young adults. Here is an instance of the impact on a client's child while getting counseled. "My parents are divorced and all my friends at school think I'm funny, crazy and happy all the time but when I get home and go to bed, I just lay there and cry for a long period, but no one knows about it. I live with my father, my three sisters and my mother lives in a different country. I love both my parents equally. I only get to see my mother in the holidays, and I miss her a lot." He is thirteen years old and his parents split up when he was four.

The impact that the split of parents has on children depends on a host of complex circumstances and situations. Some children turn out to be great if removed from conflicted environments whereas some may not, or some may stay unaffected no matter what. However, the split does have a short-term impact on children. Many suffer from lower self-esteem, anxiety, depression, poor quality contact with their parents and their standard of living decreases. These impacts linger into adulthood to have long term impact. Children may continue to have psychological difficulties or not very comfortable relationships with their parents. Most of them may end up getting divorced themselves or experience non-functional relationships influenced by their parents.

Failed relationships carve the path to a disloyal future for children. It is true that a lot of children who are raised by parents who have drifted apart due to cheating end up being unfaithful in their relationships. Parent's behavior shapes their mind. If one of the parents they are close to ends up cheating, this may cause them to think of it as acceptable behavior and they may repeat that in their relationships in the future. Betrayal between their parents can affect their psychology making them confused since they are too young to understand. A young adult may show aversion towards the cheating parent all together and their whole support system shakes. No one is born with the ability to understand a betrayer and the children may reason it to be their fault.

Alternatively, kids may seem to be ashamed of the cheating parent and may get talked about at school. Other than their parents, they are the most affected by their friends. If the lives of their parents are discussed, it makes them feel exposed. With pent up feelings back home and open discussions about their personal lives which may get indecent can adversely affect children. This gives birth to anxiety, nervous pressures, and low self-esteem. They may look for someone they can rely on and if there is a toxic environment at home and holistic environment in their school or college, they may start to act up or shut down their feelings.

When they have a fall out with their close friends, they learn to get past it. There are various issues especially in today's day and age since kids are exposed to a worldwide network, they need their parents to guide them more than ever. Children can be mean to each other and sometimes a social media post is enough to push them over the edge. This can lead to your kid overcoming the chaos and focusing on studies or other useful things.

Children may suffer from abandonment issues and act possessive and develop into insecure individuals as they grow up. The fact that they are living with a single parent or living with their stepparents can make them ache for the other parent's presence. Their fear of losing their other parent also thrives and puts a burden on everyone who later forms a friendship or relationship with them. They stop believing in love and weigh in a lot before opening up to someone. They find it extremely difficult to trust anyone. They may refuse to give any benefit of the doubt to their partners correlating it all to their parent's relationship

It has been proven how children are affected by their parent's relationship depends on the degree of the parent's conflict and how caught up they are in it. For example, if parents are fighting and the father asks his son to tell his mother that he won't be able to attend his parent's day at school. The mother responds to him through the son that why he would pass this message through him and not directly talk to her. This is when the child gets meddled in the fight and becomes a part of the conflict. This stresses them. They may even feel forced to take sides with one and lose connection with the other. For children, both parents are equally important and dear to them. They may also think that they are a reason for these constant fights between their parents and resort to self-harm.

Their trouble begins when they see their parents fight and continues through the splitting process and go further along after that. It is hard when these days divorce has become so common, and for kids to be dealing with it. In each stage of the process kids are impacted differently and they need to receive equal love and attention from both parents even if they decide to co-parent or not. Otherwise, pangs of separation will scar them for life.

If parents are constantly fighting and have a poor communication and support system in the house, children can still develop these issues. Parents need to realize that their children are a priority. They need to be sensitive to their needs and have an open conversation about their issues. They must try to avoid fighting around them and making them a part of their fights. Children should be left to worry about their school and studies rather than getting them caught up in misunderstandings at home. The rules to co-parent must be as child friendly as possible. One must not bad mouth the other person in front of them. The rest of the family members must also show the same love and care towards them devoid of the failed relationship between their parents. Leave your emotions to come together for them and raise them in a healthy and sustainable environment. Be available to answer their doubts and inhibitions. Try to obtain their validation every step of the way and explain to them suitably about what is going on around them. Share every piece of information and note their behavior around you closely. Keep in touch with their close friends' parents.

Look after your children's bodies. Their bodies tell a lot about what they are feeling. Keep an eye on their eating habits. If they complain about continuous stomach aches, they may be feeling pent up emotions and not be able to digest their food properly. An obvious reaction when a child is around his parent fighting is their heart rates increase. They may feel faint and scared. Excess stress hormones may get released which are very bad for their growth and overall health.

If either of the child's parents is emotionally available, they go through a tough time. If you are an emotionally distant father your child may lift that baggage and put it in his new relationships. He needs to heal and for this, he first needs to be aware of what kind of father he has. The father can be disapproving, mentally ill, substance-abusing, abusive, and unreliable or absent. He can be one or a combination of these traits. He should carefully note which one represents his relationship with his father. It is necessary to recall how he was treated by him as a child. He can journal his feelings, talk to his siblings or his other parent. This is necessary to stop any tease or trauma from developing or to remove an already existing one. It may be painful so it will be better for him to do this in therapy if possible. Look for the coping mechanisms he used or uses to get his father's attention. Consider which of these mechanisms are still active today. See if these are acting up to stop him from being entirely happy. Maybe he is still a workaholic or tries to go unnoticed in any situation. Think of some new ways and behavioral changes that will help him to lead a better life and suit the situation better. For example, eating disorders would have helped him get through some tough times earlier but now it's better to get past self-harming ways and live the life he deserves to live. Start with small steps. Go ahead and have lunch with the person who asks you every day and you refuse to go. Leave work early and take out time for yourself. Try to build up your courage and self-esteem. Start to talk kindly to yourself at the end of each day. Read and reread cards or letters or messages you have received over the years. Go through happy pictures you have taken with your friends. Practice self-love and try out newer things in life. Define something you held back yourself from and break free from the confines of the past.

If he had an abusive, emotionally distant or a mean mother, there are ways to heal and feel fully accepted, comforted and understood. Maybe she doesn't stay with him anymore or she has not been very receptive towards him. The truth about healing from an emotionally distant mother is that it has a lot to do with attachment. Attachment is so important for every child because it lays a safe foundation. It makes the child feel safe to go into the world and do things that seem too hard to do on his own. Not having this foundation can make you turn cold and you may find it difficult to show empathy or soothing emotions towards another person. He may become unable to express himself and when he notices someone else expressing their feelings to him, he wouldn't know how to be comforting. So, it decreases his comfort levels around anything which is emotionally driven. There is a child's voice which is innately present in everyone. His emotions are stuffed up and belted because he doesn't feel safe expressing them. This child's voice remains suppressed inside the person over all these years. So, it is necessary to find that inner voice and express everything he means to say. He can pen it down and it will be like a written letter to a child-like self to an adult self. Everything hurtful that happened or all the feelings that you had that you couldn't express or tantrum you couldn't throw. Just anything that is pent up and needs to be released from inside you. A therapy session like a safe space to do this can be so incredibly healing. He may miss a rub on the back, a warm hug or comfort of a mother's company. They can work on good mother messages that you always wanted to hear from your mother. It could be like 'I love you no matter what', 'You are so amazing' and 'I am always here for you' while doing something caring for himself. It can seem odd or even creepy, but this will make him feel a lot better in building up his support. He can visit an attachment-based trauma specialist because they can help him deal with these issues and turn them into something healthy for him. Usually, distant parents have something to do with themselves and have nothing to do with their children. If you start a conversation with them where you question their parenting and they turn defensive it can negatively impact you. So really the right way to do this is for the child to work on his relationship with himself rather than with anyone else. Engage in worrying about his well-being and trying to grow and make the best out of any situation thrown his way.

Chapter 8: After the storm the calm

After the betrayal unfolds, the relationship may end and both partners may decide to take different paths. They may also insist on staying friends, but in such cases, the relationship had seen the last of it and the betrayal was the end chapter that sealed the closing of the book. As the story ends, it is important to face and accept the situation. Sometimes ending the relationship is the best solution for both the parties. The aftermath of those devastating moments of learning about the betrayal can be manifold. Concerns arising may be about finance or a shaken support system and one of the most important decision is whether to leave or stay. The question you need to find answers to is if the relationship you are trying to save is the right one for you. Can you be happy in the relationship? Despite the current situation, do you still feel in your heart that you can take the person back? If you don't know the answers to this question, the relationship and your current situation will not be fixable.You will have problems and regret. The regret can be about either leaving them when it could have been saved or regret can be about sticking with them or emotionally challenging yourself to ultimately conclude that it can't work out anymore. How do you know if your relationship is worth it? And before that why do you want to be in the right relationship? This comes down to the real purpose of your life. Most would agree that the purpose of life is to be happy. Your relationship paves the path to your happiness. It exists because it makes you happy. Your relationship meets your needs and helps to bring out the best in you. If you are not in the right relationship, then you won't be able to be content. You won't be able to achieve your full God-given potential. Life will seem to be harder and you will always feel short of experiencing true love and well-roundedness of wellbeing.Unfulfilling relationships can lead to bad examples for your children. Therefore, it is vital to your happiness and fulfillment.

While evaluating if you are in the right relationship, it is exigent to weigh in relationship problems. These problems are catalysts that are causing emotional stress and arising doubts and confusion which may take away from what the other person means to you. You must begin by being honest to yourself. Know thyself. Be self-aware and just make an effort to know what you need in life or any relationship or a situation. Everything comes back to knowing yourself. It's not about material things that you wish to own. These things provide momentary happiness. You need to be aware of the feelings you need. How do you want to feel day to day and on a moment by moment basis? The questions you need to ask yourself for finding out what you need are what feelings are important to you. Here are some examples: happiness, security, peace, passion, intimacy, adventure, love, freedom. Think about what matters to you the most. And try to put it in one sentence about what you want to attain in your life. In other words, when you lie on your deathbed, what do you want people surrounding you to say about you? What do you want your life to have meant in the eyes of your loved ones and yourself? The next thing is to name three things that you currently want to do that will make you happy. These can be activities or anything you are involved in or affected by. Lastly, what do you think is an ideal lifestyle for you? How would you want to live ideally? It can be very different for every person. You may wish to have a penthouse in the countryside and live a simple life, being one with nature or you may desire to travel around the world. Pen down if you want to own a house or really just take care of your pets. These are some diverse examples of what ideal living means to you. When you answer all these questions you will know what you yearn for in your life.

The next step is to find your ideal partner. To know that you can step out of your current situation and enter a theoretic and ideal world. You may or may not include your current spouse in this. Paint a picture in your mind about what you feel makes your marriage fitting in making you genuinely happy. Don't put any restrictions on yourself. The picture should be about what you and your partner should be doing together and what feelings would you and your ideal partner be giving to each other. This can be very different. Some can imagine backpacking across South America where some may wish to build a business together or some may live far off in the countryside. The following step involves you to partner match. You start to match up the current partner with your ideal partner. This is going to give you an idea of whether your current partner is perfect for you not. You can move to imagine their ideal lifestyle and comparing it to yours and notice the overlap. Are you wanting the same things and more importantly the same feelings? Certain people in relationships want different things out of their marriage, so it's important to see are there any red flags. You need to see if your desires and aspirations are drastically different than your partner's it will be difficult for you to accommodate each other's needs. Usually, this mismatch causes major relationship problems such as lack of intimacy, arguments, and fights. It is necessary to be accepting of your partner's needs. If you want different things then there must be room for personal space and flexibility between them. There must be a drive to go the extra mile, compromise to reach each other's ultimate goal and create a strong reliable future together. These feelings may change from time to time so it's necessary to be in constant talks about feelings at various stages in the relationship. Identify what got both of you together in the first place. The question to face here is if you were really in love. Have you ever been in love? To generalize a few points- love is not all about chemistry or lust or initial attraction. These things change over time. You can't equate love to the lust. Love is the ability to make each other feel good and this comes through shared values. You may describe or rewind the memories of the first meeting and enunciating the feelings you felt at the time you two got together. Recount all the events not to describe them to someone else but really for yourself to evaluate what you led to you come together in the first place. Then check whether the highest values at the time for you matched that of your partner's. See if you both were looking for the same feelings. Think about your doubts, uneasy feelings or fears before entering the relationship. If so then what were those thoughts, and do you still think they are relevant? It is not uncommon to have these feelings. It's necessary to be aware of such feelings. Try to note down what is the number one reason for you getting into the relationship with this person.

Now you have to get to the current situation. You have to evaluate what feelings you have about your spouse currently. What is the real cause of all the problems between you? Are the problems clouding your true feelings for your partner? You can do this by first writing about all the things you like about your partner's personality. Identify things you like about them and things that you wish to change. After preparing a list, you need to evaluate how important is it for you to change this trait of their personality. Find how much trouble it causes you and rate it on a scale of one to ten. They don't need to change for you but you feel it is vital for you to maintain your sanity. The next step is to check how difficult will it be for your partner to change it. Since you desperately want them to change, rate this difficulty faced by them. These steps will let you understand how you feel and how your spouse feels about you and your relationship. It is also a kind of reality check about how compatible you are. Lastly, you need to ask yourself the reason for being in the relationship. What is the driving force? It can either be negative or positive. Try to think about the good reasons for being in the relationship. You need to think about their good qualities and relive good times. Think about the best qualities of your partner and see if that makes you smile internally. Acknowledge the surge or the flutter in your heart and good times you have had together. Negative reasons for staying in the relationship can be fear. You may have fears that are holding you back. Experiencing guilt, loss of face or worrying about what your family, friends or your children will think if you left or there could be financial reasons. It could be because you don't want your kids to be raised in a broken home or it could be cultural or religious reasons that forbid you to leave the person you are committed to and the most important fear of all is the fear of actually being alone and not being loved. By now, working on all these points you must have clearly understood your feelings.

On clearly knowing about your feelings, you become more alive and energized. The energy around you takes a shift. From going through life aimlessly or worried about your problems all the time you get a direction. There is almost something very distinctive about such people. They seem to be always on fire. They have a magnetic quality about them and seem to be radiant. It is a personally driven directive which makes them very compelling and confident. Usually, when a marriage or a relationship is faltering, people may feel that they have fallen out of love. Suddenly they stop feeling happy and they reason it on the marriage and their partner not being able to make them happy. They lose interest in them and confuse it to have lost the connection. At this moment you feel that leaving your partner will make you happy. However, the fact is that the failing relationship is only a symptom of the problem of not having or knowing the real purpose in life. If the person finds out what they are here for and what they are supposed to be doing, she/he will feel better about her/his life and ultimately perceive their marriage as useful. When you are not in an inspiring place in your relationship or your life, the common symptoms make you feel that your growth has stopped. But when you are on purpose you are on the verge of the steepest trajectory and at the edge of growth. There is always some kind of unfolding mystery at work. In relationships where love or attraction goes stale, usually, it is because the evolutionary edge has stopped. What compels us into relationships or business, or marriage is the purpose. The ignition or raw passion in the beginning always fades away and comes to the point of feeling like a burden or prison. There is a parallel between the raw senses of passion in the start also known as the honeymoon phase. Losing interest and that passion is the decline stage where there is no inspiration. The whole relationship seems to diffuse. So, to stop that from happening you need to divert your attention to how you are feeling currently and bring changes in your life accordingly to stay interested and focused and not get caught in the rut of the cycle of life. A lot of people have growth as their forefront goal in life where others may seek security. People in a relationship fail to realize that they are changing. When it reaches a stable point in values of growth and development in their life, they suddenly find that it's not providing them fulfillment. So, whatever gave us fulfillment early on we stop doing that and we do that without anticipating what was working. As a child learns about something, they find it extremely interesting and curious. After mastering and acquiring all the knowledge that they needed to, they move on to learning newer things. Similarly, in a relationship, there has to be something that reignites the feelings and bring you in back to the terms of what made you start the relationship. Once what was a fresh fertile soil has now become a whole landscape that has turned stale. If you need to reinvigorate, you have to reconnect with the newness.

Sex has an important part to play in this. Sex in the relationship can't be perceived as something to be done twice a week in the same way for fifty years and never get bored with it. Doing this whole thing of finding new ways to make a relationship new and doing new things together can't be easily done no matter how better you know the other person. In a healthy relationship, both of you are changing and the whole dynamic keeps changing. It takes a lot of effort and focuses to keep the momentum going. There is, for instance, a large number of people who change their jobs multiple times before they take a steady job. There is a rapid change that goes on. It is a metamorphic phenomenon and this centers around our mastery on each level of the game. Things may start to lose their edge a little. But then new edges appear, and growth continues. When you retrospectively map someone's career, you notice that due to some reason you stopped and moved on to the next best option. This is the real progression and when we apply it in our lives every day, you shouldn't refrain from using the same in your relationships. You need to sharpen your awareness to follow this thread. This also casts light on pressures put on people from society. The instant gratification that you will be happier if you get this or that or perhaps moving in the same direction as others are moving in. The whole cycle of ego and wishing life speeds up is quickening. We are always in an unprecedented territory because all the rules about relationships no longer seem to apply and we have much higher expectations about what we want from our relationship.

We want the higher things from relationships and that too continually and once these emotional needs are met, we start to question things. If you are being divorced or you are trying to pull away from a person, there is nothing more important for you to do than to get on a purpose. Purpose makes you attractive. Hartville Hendricks described something called isolate user dynamic. Isolator fuse dynamic is one person doing the running and the other person doing the chasing. Isolator unconsciously pushes others away and keep people at a distance because they need a lot of space around them. Freedom is very important to them. The fuser is the one who has an insatiable need for closeness. Fusers want to do things together all the time. If people fail to meet them on time, they start to feel abandoned. The thought of divorce makes them cry. They crave physical affection and reassurance and they need to stand in close verbal contact. We can sometimes switch roles. There is a lot of flexibility from just calling yourself a fuser type or isolate type. Various relationships can bring out aspects of ourselves. The fuser energy is more aligned with feminine energy inside the system and isolate is mostly aligned with the masculine. Though all of us have both. But the two are very different drivers. The core principle behind feminine energy is love. The females will remain largely unfulfilled until it comes to know itself as love. The masculine principle, which is internally embedded in us, the primary energy behind it is a purpose. The purpose is greater than itself and it remains unfulfilled unless it is ignited by another purpose. When you have someone in your life playing the fuser role, they are a little more oriented in the love or heart space whereas the isolate partner is out in the world and their focus is on the partner or carrier or business or just anything. The fuser needs to get on purpose. The part of what makes the isolate so attractive is their attention is not on the fuser. They are aligned with their things. It is carved off and making them unavailable. This is exactly what the fuser needs to be doing. To get connected with yourself to achieve this, you need to do several things. Recognize yourself in that fuser role where you are the one who is chasing, and your partner is running. Their attention is not on you or your family. There is something that they are compelled to do which is the other person. You realize the attention is going elsewhere. Getting in touch with the isolator quality will provide you strength. Your sense of sense will get stronger and less reliant on your isolator. You will feel like a brick around them as opposed to how you would feel like a wreck. The effect of the way they are treating you won't affect you as much and you may experience a backbone building that will aid you in standing alone. Your partner is going to experience this shift, and this may make them wish to come back in and reconnect. Therefore, it is critical to get on purpose.

If you are putting a lot of effort to get back with the person and you are doing everything you can to keep the relationship together and the other person is just not responding, and they are still insisting on leaving you, they are still ignoring you or treating you badly, they may also be refusing communication or they could even be carrying on with an affair which can be either emotional or physical. If you are in this situation, it is very easy to be despondent and disheartened and even more upset with the whole situation. The whole thing doesn't seem fair. It may seem like you are making all the effort and the other person is carrying on without any sign of consideration for you. There are a few things that you can do in this situation. The first thing to realize is that if you have a spouse who wants to go away and you want to stay together you are facing one of the most difficult situations you could ever face. You both want different things right now. As you both moved forward in your relationship since the inception, things have changed. We may sometimes forget about this, but change is a fact of life. Everything in the world is in a constant state of change. So, your spouse has changed, and the situation of your relationship has changed. Sometimes conflicts arise in the relationship and we resist to change according to the circumstances. This resistance may have been caused by not accepting the changes. We prefer things remaining the same way they have been. We may look back and feel things were better than they probably were. But we find it difficult to accept that things are different. So, the first step is to accept that both you and your partner has changed and there is nothing wrong with that. It is perfectly natural. You need to take away the expectation that they should want to stay married to you. Because you expect them to be loving and if you have a great relationship just like you had in the past you are only going to put pressure on them and make them feel bad. When you put pressure on them that is the fastest way to drive someone away from the relationship. Keep reminding yourself that expectations mean more pressure and that pressure will push your partner farther away. But how can this be done without actually feeling disappointed when they refuse to accommodate your needs? You need to remember how things are going is the best for your marriage. You have feelings and you wish to have a great relationship because you love them. But by making a few changes yourself, you can make them interested in staying with you and take the pressures that are pushing them away out of your relationship. Get rid of the feeling that you need to stay in a relationship or stay married to this person in your life to stay happy. Of course, you want to be together with them and you want to feel all the good things of having them in your life. But it is possible to leave them, say if your life depended on it. It could be possible for you to find someone else to have a happy relationship with. But you don't want to do that but you could if you had to. So, you don't need your spouse to be happy. When you get it, you will be amazed just how happy you start to feel. Nothing would have changed on the outside. You would still be married, you might be in the current situation with all the bad but you would have evolved on the inside. The ultimate truth is when things start to change on the inside, then they begin to change on the outside. So ultimately, you want to stay together and you want the things to work out but you don't need to be with them. This takes a lot of pressure on the relationships especially at a sensitive time like this. Next, you need to start focusing on yourself. Ask yourself how you can be happy. We often forget when things get out of touch in our relationship, we habit ourselves into remaining upset and try to work hard to fix our problems. We are trying so hard to keep our partner happy that we forget about our own happiness. Don't tell yourself that once your relationship is healed and you both are back together you will be happy. You need to feel that you don't need the relationship to make you happy. You are enough. Make a list of things that you can do at the moment that will make you happy. This is a kind of reassurance that you don't need your partner to be happy at this moment. Start doing them almost immediately to feel good. Don't think that's selfish on your part to do something that's keeping your mood light at this problematic time. Imagine if you ever see your children or someone who you love being happy, would you tell them to stop because they should rather focus on their problems or would you just be glad to see them happy? Then why not treat yourself with the same love and respect? You deserve to be in a happy place in your life. Another step in the process of healing from your uncooperative partner is to allow them to make mistakes. They might go off to do stupid things. They might have an affair, they may start texting someone something inappropriate, they might yell at you, they might ask for a divorce. They are saying this because everybody makes mistakes including you. We start expecting them to be perfect and not make any mistakes at all, however that is not a part of being a human being. Then you need to work on changing the meaning of what's hurting you. If you are feeling hurt, it doesn't necessarily come from someone else or what someone else has done to you. It comes from what you think about that person's actions. It's about what you perceive their actions to mean. You have different expectations about what that person should or shouldn't have done. A person may say that he is hurt because his wife cheated on him and she shouldn't have done that. The wife may respond by saying he should not have been so cold towards her. He should have considered my feelings. But think, why should they consider your emotions? People are truly doing only one thing in their entire life which is trying to be happy. So instead of reacting, being hurt, saying my husband or wife should make amends, ask yourself a different and much more powerful question- I wonder why they have done it. Is there anything I can do to help? See if you can find a different meaning for your behavior. And lastly, give it some time. Things take time to work and things are going to change. The situation right now is not permanent. They won't continue to act in this way forever. Soon you will have to make a decision-if you want to keep trying or if you have had enough? This is not possible to say in general terms how long it will take for your relationship to get back to normal or will it ever reach the point that you both are happy together again. But it's paramount that you value yourself. Work on your own happiness first.

Chapter 9 "What to do to get happy again"

A question that haunts the mind of the betrayed is whether the unfaithful person ever regrets their decision. Whether they will ever miss them or just easily move on with someone else after they have made them suffer miserably. Usually the betrayed feels like they are the only mourners of the relationship. Society will judge them because everyone will think they could not provide something to the other person that made them leave them. But the unfaithful suffer too. They might not be communicating it, but it is true. The most important thing that the betrayed needs to do to be completely happy again is to leave the will to seek revenge. You need to understand that your partner is not a sociopath. They may be portraying that they are unaffected but life has a way of coming full circle. They will have their accountability and suffering that they would need to deal with at their end. As this quote by Tim

Keller rightly points, "We have to release the urge to exact the payment from the other and make them hurt how we hurt and feel what we feel if we truly want to forgive." Therefore, forgiveness is paramount to the journey. Everyone has their path that they choose for themselves. If someone decides to leave you, it is their choice, even though it is extremely selfish. But if they stay together then you both will be miserable.

When you are upset over getting dumped and you beat yourself up for falling for that person, keep breathing. Tolerate the hurt and try to find your new normal self. You are allowed to whine and sulk in front of people who surround you. Focus on your feelings. Attempt to comprehend what it is that hurts the most. If you don't fully know what is causing the hurt, you won't be able to overcome and move on. You may be bent out of shape due to your loss. You don't feel like you are good at getting anything done and the loss has left a mark. You may feel that you are not interested in and capable of finding love again. These feelings make you vulnerable. There is a contradiction in your mind whether you would have been happy if you were still together with that person. At this moment you might even forget about the abuse and neglect or betrayal that you faced while being in the relationship. The anger about losing your dignity and value hits hard. But it is necessary to acknowledge there is a loss. To enter into the next phase of your life and to be happy, you need to face this loss. Without being aware of it you can never finish your feelings for them. Therefore, forgiving the person is paramount to a healthy life. The unfaithful have their moments of incredible shame and humiliation too. It is not easy for anyone to get away with their wrongdoings. It comes back to them or it may already be haunting them. Just to not lose face they may be acting stronger, aloof or unaffected.

One of the prominent differences between being in a happy relationship than in a failing one is how couples deal with mistakes. We all make mistakes. Somehow, we believe that people in perfect marriages or relationships never make mistakes. They don't have any problems. They are different and better people than the rest of us. The truth of the matter is people who are in great marriages still make a lot of mistakes. They may even make more mistakes, but the real distinguishing factor is in how they deal with them. The meaning they attach to mistakes is different than others. There are certain things that you can do to attach a different meaning to mistakes in your relationship so you can deal with them in a much better way. The quality of your love depends on what you think making a mistake means to you. It is irrespective of how big we feel the mistake is. It could be a major mistake like betraying your partner, but it can also be smaller things that impact your relationship negatively. It could be losing your temper, getting angry and shouting at your spouse or being cold and non-communicative with them or refusing to consider their feelings. How we look at mistakes can have a very devastating effect. It can cause a lot of stress and strain in the relationship. They keep your relationship stuck in a negative space. Whatever you focus on, you will get more of it. If you focus on trying to get over something or trying to heal from a mistake, you are going to get more and need to put in more effort and time. It may also drive a person to make more mistakes. Any person who is weak in a relationship is unattractive. If you have made a mistake and you are making an effort to make everything better, you start to feel bad about yourself. You are being weak. You are not going to be attractive to your spouse. If you have made a mistake and are dwelling on it or you are trying to heal yourself or your spouse from it, it is going to have the opposite effect. Reacting to a mistake in the wrong way can offend and create an imbalance in power. If you are the perpetrator and your partner is the victim, it creates inequality between both. It takes the couple away from one place that they want to be in. You both want to be in a happy and easy, fun-loving space in your relationship now. Mistakes are made in the past and if you keep focusing on overcoming them it keeps you in the past. The dictionary definition of a mistake is an error or fault resulting from defective judgment, deficient knowledge or carelessness. Defective means not being perfect.

Everyone most commonly forgets that no one is perfect. Being defective is an integral part of being a human being. It's natural to make mistakes. Then deficient knowledge can be interpreted as mistakes that come from a result of things that we simply don't know. If we don't know how to react in a situation or to a particular event because it might be a new experience, we won't know the right thing to do. No one has perfect knowledge. We can also make mistakes when we are not careful and not paying attention and simply being careless. The consequence of doing something rash like losing your temper or even connecting inappropriately with the third person like having a physical or emotional affair is difficult to undo but our minds can be clouded by our emotions. We are not using our logical mind at this point to make our decisions. There are a few things that do not come under the ambit of the word 'mistake'. First if a mistake isn't intentional. It is not something that is done intentionally and out of spite for our partner. We can't imagine the consequences, so it's not intended. The mistake made is not permanent, it might have been a single incident or could have been repeated multiple times such as developing a negative attitude towards your spouse. The damage occurs when we stick to it. We realize its beginning but don't want to see the end of it. We keep the memory of the mistake and that is just internally harming ourown heart and soul. So, the mistake has ended but we are stuck in the damage it has caused.

Acknowledge that you have made a mistake, both to yourself and your partner. You don't need to justify yourself or come up with reasons or any long analysis of why you acted the way that you did. Just say it to yourself and to your spouse that you made a mistake and that you are sorry. The next important thing is to stop apologizing. Once is enough. Stop continually reminding the partner that you or they made a mistake by either apologizing or by complaining about it. It won't make any positive difference. It is distracting you from thinking what you are supposed to think and feel at the moment. Stop being responsible for your partner's feelings. The moment anyone takes responsibility for someone else' feelings, they will never achieve true harmony in the relationship. We need to take full responsibility for our feelings. It takes you away from attaining the basic goal of happiness and fulfillment in your life. It might be hard. They might be angry with you and they could be blaming you and make you feel guilty. They might even threaten your relationship. But it is their problem. You are not going to see any true progress towards creating a really happy marriage until you and your spouse start learning to take responsibility for your feelings. You both are adults and you both can learn to be more self-aware. So, don't keep taking this responsibility away from them and allow them to learn how to be responsible for their feelings. If that's all that you do in your relationship it will seem to genuinely transform. Try to see the other side of making mistakes. Just focus on what was the good that the mistake brought to you. What has your mistake or your partner's mistake taught you? How can you use it to improve your relationship? What good things can now happen in the relationship as a result of having made the mistake? Mistakes are small reminders of what is not right between a couple. If you do not take the mistake as a warning and you perhaps carry on doing it, this can have a disastrous effect on your marriage. What is the positive side of having an affair? Probably it has made you realize that you have lost the fun and intimacy in your marriage and you have stopped doing those things together that made the relationship fun, or you have stopped appreciating your husband/wife for the wonderful people they are. It is like a wake-up call. It calls for a lot of awareness and effort to make those things right rather than just letting the marriage or relationship slide away. You need to create a new meaning for the word mistake. Calling a mistake an error or a fault is quite negative. It sounds like something you are doing wrong. The definition that successful marriages have or some great people have is that a mistake is a learning opportunity and a gift that you have been given to make your life better. If you see your mistakes this way, you will feel there is a huge opportunity to learn and grow and improve your life. It will make you and your partner a better person. Expect to make more mistakes. Look forward to making more mistakes. People who have this mentality see things more positively. It gets wired into your brain. You gleam with positivity since the negative definition of calling a mistake an error is now delightfully called an opportunity to sprout. For instance, Thomas Edison tried multiple times to make a bulb., after several attempts. He was asked by reporters if he ever felt discouraged after failing. He said he couldn't imagine it working. The real wonder was when he made the discovery. This attitude of accepting and embracing your flaws can take you places in your relationship and cement the foundation of your relationship no matter what the mistakes that plague it. It is not actually what happens that determines how happy you are, but it is about the meaning we attach to the things happening around us. If you change the meaning that you have attached to your partner's past mistakes you are going to start to act differently. You will get different results.

Can you save your relationship when your partner has already left? Can it be saved if they are seeking a divorce? If you are in a situation where your husband or your wife has packed their bags and moved out and filed for divorce, it is very devastating. It brings a sense of reality to the fact that your marriage really might be over. You may have talked about ending your marriage for weeks or months. You might have tried extremely hard for them to stay by counseling or making amends. It feels like the end of the dreams and memories that you shared and the things in the future that you wanted to share with them as well. You start to make decisions about your life and future. You are single again. Accept where you are right now and how you are taking it. You feel terrible and life looks bleak. It's important not to deny or fight. You are feeling lonely and things aren't good. The next thing to realize is it's never too late to save your marriage. People get together with their partners after weeks, months or even years after being separated. People even get divorced and remarry someone else and then get back together. So, the bottom line is it is never too late to save your marriage or relationship. The reason why you can't save your relationship is when you decide you don't want to save the marriage. As time goes on you realize you are much happy without that person as you were with them. You are finding you're capable of finding greater happiness with someone else or somewhere else. It is the most important outcome of your life that you are happy. The other reason is that you give up. If your husband/wife loved you once, they can love you again. Even if more people come into their lives and different things happen that upset you but the emotions that your partner felt for you once can be felt again.

Some things that you can do to move your partner in your direction, despite them having left you are you should not panic. It is a very hard and stressful time. They have already left your sight. You will need to be in a far stronger place to make things work without giving up and without finding your happiness somewhere else. You will have to make better decisions. Stop looking backwards. If you start to question where you are now by looking back at what went wrong in the relationship, you will be creating negative feelings. You will create blame, shame, guilt, anger, resentment or depression. None of them will help your situation but make things rather worse. Start looking forward into your future. This means focus on the future that you want to have. You want to be happily married or stay together with your partner. Thinking about this doesn't help to achieve it. But it does make you positive and hopeful. It sends you to a much better place to get your husband/wife back. Be positive when you are around them. You must be cheerful, upbeat, pleasant and optimistic. It doesn't mean to give them everything they say they want or to become week. It doesn't mean that you condone or forgive their behavior. It just means that you don't allow any negative feelings or energy to creep into any dealings that you have with them. This is very hard to do. Your behavior is going to make a big impression on them. The positivity is going to rub off on them and make a big difference. Lastly, you need to pick yourself up and get out of your current situation. Pick up a new hobby and do new things. Surround yourself with people who will make you feel good. Try to take some action to create a positive future. You will feel much better. It is very rewarding to take control of your life. With great things happening in your life, you will begin to feel better. You may also start enjoying yourself too much and think that you are happier without being married to your husband/wife. For some people, divorce becomes the best thing that's ever happened to them. They later think about how they ever imagined being happy with that person. If you thought you were happy, now you are realizing the true meaning of being happy. This is not suggesting that you have this outcome nor should you look at this outcome and judge your situation. But when you focus on your happiness, you are going to start to feel better. Who you are is very attractive and when you live by being honest and true to yourself, you become attractive to the world. When the estranged spouse sees you living a happy life they start to find you much more attractive than they ever did. They may start asking themselves what they are missing out on. They may start to miss being a part of your great life. People have had very messy divorces and very tragic things happening to them in their lives. But these people would agree that the worst things that happened to them, actually turned out to be the best thing that could have ever happened to them. Your struggles make you grow and help you get stronger. You start to live through your true self rather than just living through. You may struggle with your fears. The better the person we are, the better the life you are going to have. The more you deal with adversity the better the person you become. You then attract a better life for yourself. So, a lot of it has to do with your mental attitude, your beliefs and strength you build in your mind.

You can be in three situations. First is when you forgive your spouse and you are ready to reconcile with them. It's much likely that you end up back together. You may reconcile but are unable to forgive them. This is the place where you are stuck in negative thoughts and you must try to pass through that hallway of bitterness and come to face the facts. The next phase is when you have forgiven but haven't reconciled. This is the time when you are just waiting for that last push, a sign from the universe or a lifejacket to make you get through the passage and summon the strength to get back with your partner. Deep inside you, you have forgiven them and are either reluctant to take them back or you are waiting for them to repent more and then take them back. The last situation you can find yourself in is when you neither reconcile nor forgive. This is sadly the end of the relationship. You or your spouse may run to the lawyers and file for divorce. No matter what situation you are in, learning to place your happiness above everything else is the most important. Understand this to be a wake-up call to start paying more attention and care to yourself.

Chapter 10: Examples for setting up a shooting path

Here are a few examples of situations that people have faced in their lives and what they can do to heal or react after finding out.

"He cheated on me and was unable to take responsibility for his actions or even admit it for that matter until I kept questioning him. I found out he cheated with two other women and he made the same excuses and now he is trying to get back together with me and is claiming he is a different person."

It is mostly construed that the betrayed is the only one in pain and needs to be healed. However, the offender may also shut down due to the guilt of cheating and to cope with this they may end up blaming the other person. The narcissistic behavior may be caused due to certain events in their past or just their nature of fearing commitment. This has nothing to do with the betrayed. The betrayed must try to be aware of their emotions and feelings. The rage and the grief of losing someone they cared so much about should be patiently understood and dealt with. If this person returns after causing all the trauma, check if the person is remorseful and don't rush into anything. Take it slow and maintain a continuous stream of conversations and discuss or point out any oddities you face in each other's behavior.

"I've been cheated on, lied to and abused by my ex-fiancé. I was 7 months pregnant with our daughter. One month after I gave birth I learned about his affair. He kept on denying it until he admitted the affair when he went back to his work on a cruise ship. It really hurts because we've been in a committed relationship for eleven years. He blamed everything on me. And he even dared to deny that he is the father. I told him no one had ever touched me except him and I'm willing to have my daughter undergo a DNA test to prove to him that he's the father. He kept accusing me of cheating on him when in fact he's the one who cheated."

This is extremely excruciating. Having a child while facing this situation makes it extremely hard to cope with. The first thing that needs to be done is to get help or get in touch with your family or some trusted person. The recent abandonment and indifference of the partner can be too much to handle. An expecting woman is already at a sensitive time in her life. So, the priority must be to lose correspondence with this cheating partner and find a safe environment where you are nurtured and loved. Having a child assures companionship for life. This is precious. Even if the other person has the thought of shrugging all responsibilities, you are enough. Visit a psychiatrist and have good and long therapeutic sessions to release inner emotions. Finance can be a big factor especially when an infant is involved. Sort your life out with the help of your loved ones and try to put your focus away from anything that reminds you of them.

"When the mask slipped on my covert ex-wife and she left me and the children, I had no clue as to why. She was drinking and staying away from home and I thought that alcohol was the issue. As a consequence of my divorce, I discovered that my mother was a covertly narcissistic and my ex-wife was one as well. My ex-wife never gave me any concrete reason why she left other than I "didn't change." What was I supposed to change into? A butterfly? It made no sense."

Women want emotional support, fairness, friendship, and sensitivity in their relationship. Even though this seems a lot but when you are entering into a relationship with a person, it is necessary to know and understand the person. A woman wants a man to have a good heart and work hard in the relationship. It may even be about having money or being attractive. She wants someone who loves her unconditionally who she can love back. However, it is necessary to look for signs if a person is dissatisfied with you. Any relationship no matter how compatible will suffer issues if couples don't talk about their feelings and emotions openly to each other. Ignoring one another while in the relationship only increases the distance between the partners. It is hard but the key is to actually understand what the other person expects of you and making a decision based on the possibility of fulfilling their expectations. Otherwise, it is a waste of time for both people.

"My boyfriend of three years told me he had been cheating on me for the last few months with some girl both physically and emotionally. He said he wasn't happy with me and that's why he did it. I did everything in the world to make this man happy. I was there for him through so much, including the passing of his mother. Most of our arguments centered on him always going out with friends, clubbing, drinking, and not spending enough time with me and making me feel special. He pointed out how "annoying and needy" I was when I asked for more in the relationship, which in turn caused him to be unhappy and seek out this other woman. I had this gut feeling all along and he told me I was crazy and couldn't be more wrong and he repeatedly denied there was anything going on with them. Now I can't help but wonder how he gave everything we shared away to some other girl so easily."

After finding out about the person who you cared about so much and whose life you invested in turn away from you is unbearable. It can crush the nervous system of any person and it's very common to feel belittled and dumb. The gush of emotions engulfing you can get the best of you. For the victim who is hurt, it is necessary to think about the moments in the relationship when the other person reciprocated their emotions. More likely than not, if the betrayed reflects they may find out that the other person never showed the same level of affection and care as they did. The imbalance can make a person take you for granted and may construe you to be something of a pushover. This usually surfaces only after the shock of betrayal. The person who has gone out of the relationship starts to fear commitment because they are too present for them. This is completely the offender's fault who is not clearly viewing the person in the same light as they are. Their real fault is they could have ended the relationship by being transparent rather than cheating and then summoning the audacity to reveal their affair and blame the other person. The victim should have looked for signs of cheating earlier and if nothing seemed suspicious, then such person is an obsessive cheater and no matter how attached they are, they are most likely to cheat repeatedly. The victim needs to accept the fact to finally move on and refrain from letting self-doubt to clog their minds.

"Years ago, I was deeply in love with a guy and I thought that we would get married. When he left me, I honestly thought that I would die. I even considered suicide. It took me three years to get over him. I am now married to a wonderful man and I am happy. I rarely think about my ex these days, and I know that I have forgiven him because I don't hate him anymore. I hope that he has found as much happiness as I have. It's a cliché, but it is so true that time is a healer."

Time truly heals. It's about attaining maturity and controlling your emotions from getting the best of you in the situation. Once your partner cheats, the adrenaline rush that flows through the body makes them either shut down or become violently aggressive. You can get drawn into these emotions and may get as down as wishing to end your life. But what is important is at those moments you just hold on to something positive in you. It shouldn't be external, it has to be internal. A strong mind and a drive to live a better life independently must motivate you to reach a better phase in your life. Take this as an experience where you learn something and not let it paralyze or scar you for good. This is not the only relationship that you will have in your life. You need to work towards getting your confidence back and know your worth. No one should be so important that they claim a right over your life. Everyone is sufficient for themselves. The feeling of ending up alone is an irrational fear that the mind creates, and the other person becomes irreplaceable. However, they can be replaced by someone capable of loving you even more than them and you can have the life you deserve with them.

"Getting cheated on by the person who talks about how much they love you is the worst thing ever. Although I've been cheated on once by the person I adore, I found it in my heart to give him another chance and as time passes by, we've been doing way much better. Communication and understanding and love are much stronger."

Marriage is not easy. Even if it is a happy one, there is no manual on how to navigate through all the challenges that will come your way. Couples have to learn each other's needs and basic nature and most importantly communicate well. Communicating may sometimes be too hard to do but the better the communication, the lesser is the build-up and the lesser fights. It is a personal choice to take back a person who cheated on you. It must be a well-rounded decision and must be done for all the right reasons. To stay together amidst societal pressures is not a good idea. This can hamper everyone who surrounds them- their family members, friends or children. Coming together because there is a lot of love between two people and due to some reason one swayed, but their love for each other is too difficult to ignore. They are emotionally too dependent and happy that they are ready to work on the differences. Transparency is promised and kept and communication about any issues faced by either are welcomed and discussed properly.

"I can only talk for myself, it took three years to forgive and five years to regain trust. Even then it can only be achieved if the person that cheated shows genuine remorse, which in my case was very strong."

It is wrong to completely think that the relationship is surely over after one cheats on another. Betrayal can be one of the most difficult things to get over in a relationship. A third person who enters the relationship is now forming a part of the dynamics and it is difficult to get past that feeling of your loved one allowing someone else to enter your marriage. However, it is possible to make amends. The support system has to be rebuilt. Trust needs to be regained and ensured that they will never go outside the relationship again. It is very difficult to form trust and surpass the pain. However, with full disclosure and by providing a safer environment for the other person, this can be achieved.

Chapter 11: I still believe in our relationship

You don't want to let go. You still have faith in the relationship. You wish to get your partner to forgive you and get rid of the resentment they have towards you and you want to give your marriage a chance. This becomes difficult. The spouse can't seem to forgive you and can't get over the hurt they are feeling. The first step in rebuilding the relationship is to get over this hurt and resentment. It can be caused by your affair or humiliating them in public in some way or due to some specific behavior that you displayed to them. The resentment towards you has something to do with what you have done to them in the past as a reaction to which they are still treating you in a disrespectful way. You may not have cared about their feelings. It can even be mental or physical abuse or lack of intimacy. People gets focused on stressful points in their lives and tend to neglect their spouse. They have a tendency to shut down in front of you. They stop responding to you emotionally. There can be a lack of communication. One of the prime reasons that's causing these negative feelings to grow is lack of intimacy. This includes sex and also simple affection. Perhaps your partner doesn't want to touch or doesn't want to be touched or hugged or kissed. Sometimes spouses tell them that they are physically repulsed by them. This is the ultimate sign of hurt and lack of forgiveness. They may start to put other things ahead of you in the relationship. They feel other things are of a higher priority. It can be their children, other family members or friends or even their hobbies, interests or jobs, their business or their career. Ideally, the relationship must one of the highest-ranking priorities in both people's lives. They may intentionally hurt the other person and it may seem impossible for you to make them forgive you. They may be alienating you from your children or close friends or family members. Many may start to overspend. This is called financial sabotage. They intend to cause hurt to the other person in lieu if the hurt is caused to them by the other person. The consequences can be quite extreme where it can even end up with a person developing personality disorders. So, this creates a barrier between the two of you. It makes communication, trust, and intimacy almost impossible. Therefore, you need to eliminate these barriers in order to move forward. Another thing that may be triggered is that it causes you to behave in the same way. You may also start holding back and emotionally shut down. Check your partner's behavior and begin to analyze the pattern of resentment that they are displaying. This can give you clues on how to deal with it. First is when your partner wants to forgive you but doesn't know how. They recognize they are hurting, and they can't forgive you. They know their behavior isn't helping you but genuinely don't know what to do about it. The way to know this is to ask yourself, is your partner aware that they can't forgive you? Does the inability to forgive make them feel bad? Does it appear that they seriously want to do something about it and they want to get over the hurt and resentment feelings towards you and they are assuming some responsibility in trying to do this? The other type of resentment which is fairly common is when they don't want to forgive you. Even if they say they want to. They are in such a position that they use their apparent pain to punish the other person. They are saying you hurt me. I won't forgive you until you receive some punishment. So, they will punish you by staying hurt because they know that hurts you too. This is a very prevalent belief that people have. It is a way of maintaining control over you and the relationship. They are meaning to tell you how you feel, and this can take a destructive turn. You need to ask yourself, are they in a place where they can ever actually forgive you? You will be able to answer this easily based on their behavior and feelings and actions.

True forgiveness is removing all the pain and traces of the pain from the outer world and the inner world as well. To forgive you completely they need to get rid of all the remains of the pain surrounding what caused the hurt. It has to be unconditional. They have to say it doesn't matter what happens, they are going to let go and come back to you. It is acknowledging what happened and then sticking together and not letting the emotions of abandoning the person overpower you. This is the ultimate goal. It is achievable. Let's begin by stating that you must be sorry for what you did wrong or whoever did wrong must have repented in their heart. That behavior needs to stop. If you had an affair, you need to stop everything you had with that person. You can't realistically expect to not be apologetic and your partner to forgive you and you may even keep repeating what caused a rift between you. If the husband goes and cheats and the wife forgives, after half a dozen times, she stops forgiving and he wonders why is she no longer forgiving me and is cynical. There has to be genuine remorse and a genuine want to not hurt the person anymore. If you do have a pattern of repeating what causes your partner to get hurt, you need to identify the cause that's stirring you to do it. You need to repair that element. It's not about dealing with forgiveness, it's about dealing with the pattern. Certain myths need to be busted when dealing with the grey area. To think that time will heal, and the relationship will restore to its formal glory. This is true to some extent. This can often be used as an excuse by a person to not do much. The person just wallows in self-pity. Like any change, healing from hurt can be done instantly. They would need to have deeply and truly forgiven the other person. To do that there has to be the right environment and the right mindset and you can heal fairly quickly. You need to give it as much time as it needs. The process can be sped up depending on what you do and how you do it. Another myth is it is up to them to deal with it. It's their problem to deal with and you leave them and let yourself have time to soak it in and decide what you want to do. Getting them to take responsibility is certainly important. The problem is if you leave it for them to deal with it they might not know what to do and the timeframe is going to be based on their time frame. You are not giving them any support. It should be explained that it is up to them to deal with the situation, but you are there to help and support them every step of the way. You are waiting for them to come back. But this shouldn't be misconstrued as you apologizing, all the time and crowding them. This will have a repellent effect. So, you need to find a balance to deal with the situation effectively. You are giving all of your power to them. What they need to get over the pain and hurt is some strength. You are making yourself weak which is in turn, making the whole situation weak. There is nothing to pull them up here.

What can you do to try to get them to forgive you? Make sure to not take responsibility for their feelings. Your spouse needs to take responsibility for their feelings. They may not want to or may say that they can't. But true healing and forgiveness can never happen if it is not coming to them internally. The way to do this is telling them that you are sorry, and you are ready to take responsibility. You will make sure it doesn't happen again but ultimately, it's up to you to be completely transparent. You can say you love them, and you want to help but you can't force them to forgive you. They need to take responsibility for that. Next is to forgive yourself.

You may have baggage on your shoulders and the guilt is eating you up inside and you may lose face and sleep. You did make a mistake. You are human. Everyone makes mistakes. This is not to negate the mistake in any sense. Accept and forgive yourself for that. You have assured them and yourself that it is never going to happen again. Make sure you are doing your best that it never happens again. Don't feel guilty. Guilt never does any good for anyone. Next, you need to acknowledge and resolve. Acknowledge to your partner that you did them wrong and tell them that is completely your wish to heal the relationship. It will be made better and will get back to what it was. Whatever happened has happened but do this powerfully and firmly so that they know you mean business. At this point, it won't be advisable to ask them how they feel. They have done that over and over and revealed to you how sick they are feeling. Tell them how you feel. You are hopeful and willing to make amends. You resolve that things will change for the better and they will be better. The next step is to ask them to acknowledge that you are both human and you both are capable of making mistakes. Do this in a general and non-confrontational way. You tell them that you have acknowledged what you have done, and you resolve that you want things to get better. But isn't it true that you both are human. You have made mistakes, but they make mistakes too. You are not accusing them, but you are reminding them in a non-confrontational way. What you are doing is that you are getting them to agree to another side of what happened. There are always two sides to everything. This is why the blame game never works. People can't always see another side to everything. The effect of what you are doing here will diffuse some of the resentment and rationalize their fears a little bit. They might begin to see it's not fully your fault. You made a mistake and it's not the end of the world. The last step lies to create a positive healing environment. When we have a lot of problems in the relationship, that's what we are focused on. It just creates an endless cycle of problems, hurt, pain and misery. It's no wonder people don't want to be there. This way we are just focusing on the bad stuff. Now that you have acknowledged it's their responsibility and resolved their hurt and forgiven yourself, this step is about moving on. You don't need to focus on this stuff anymore. Focus on creating a positive environment. Refuse to focus on the negative. Whatever you wish to achieve that's what you get. If you want to heal things, just focus on the positives. The correct way to do to is if they seem upset, don't apologize. You give them support but don't continue to say sorry to them. Just move the focus away from that. Another way is to be attractive. Show your mental strength. If you are happy and optimistic, you are not being cynical. You have acknowledged you made a mistake. Now you can be happy and optimistic about the future. Don't dwell on the problems. It is necessary to be loving towards your partner but not in a weak way. You need to restore your pre affair state of affairs. Don't react to negativity. Tell them that you love them, but you are not going to react to the negativity. That's the greatest gift you can give to anybody that they are responsible for their feelings. You worry about how you feel and let them worry about how they feel.

The harsh reality is that about 44% of married men and 34% of married women have had affairs in their lives. The younger you are the more likely you are to have an affair. It can happen at any stage. It is quite common to have these affairs. Is honesty a far-fetched concept? How important is honesty in any relationship? It's obvious. It is something that we learned since our childhood that honesty is the best policy. It is about telling the truth and not telling any lies. It has a much deeper and powerful meaning in a relationship. In a relationship, it means two people living their true and authentic selves without fear of the consequences. It involves the other person to do the same unconditionally. First and foremost, are you living an authentic life? Are you being who you are? Take an example of someone you admire. What distinguishes them from the rest of us? I think one of the reasons why we get attracted to such people is that they are living their true life irrespective of any criticism or negativity from others. They are being themselves and they are happy to be themselves. Not having fear of the consequences is detrimental to any relationship. Something that holds us back in our relationship is usually based on our fears. The fear of what we might feel can happen, fear of being criticized or being hurt or making mistakes. We have to get to a place where there is no fear of real honesty to start happening. See if it is allowing the other person to do the same unconditionally. It means not just being yourself but allowing the other person to be themselves too. Allow them to make their own mistakes so that they know what is true to them without being offended or hurt by it. Can you imagine being in the relationship and being able to say anything you wanted and not intentionally wanting to hurt the other person? If you can and you feel you will never be judged by them for that and you can live your life developing yourself, imagine the huge positive impact that is going to have on yourself and everyone else around you. If you are facing the fear that your partner is not being completely honest with you, the place to start even in that situation is yourself. You need to ask yourself honest questions. Why do you think they are not being honest with you? Are they able to express the feelings to you without the fear of consequences? Are you living your true self without any fear?

Maybe in a relationship you are still unaware of the depth of honesty that you can achieve. This can make a big difference in the quality of your relationship. Ask yourself these questions- Are you able to share every thought you ever had with them? Are there any thoughts that you haven't been able to share with them? However big or small. If your spouse asks you what you are doing or thinking, are you always totally honest with them? Have you ever not said something to your spouse, but you are thinking about it? Have you had a sexual fantasy more than once and will you be able to tell your spouse about it? Can you explain it to them in great detail without getting embarrassed? And not find this too daunting. There are very few honest marriages. Don't feel bad if you aren't there because you are not alone. The first step is to identify your standing and the extent of honesty you both share. If you are not living in a relationship based on total honesty, you will feel caged. You can't be completely happy because you are bottling up your feelings and not letting them out. There are consequences for your spouse when you are not completely honest to them. They are going to be frustrated and confused. There will be miscommunication between you due to the reluctance in speaking from your heart out to each other. The whole thing of shared growth is going to be lacking from the relationship. You need to have the liberty to make mistakes and learn from them. If you are unable to do that you are going to reach a saturation point and the relationship won't be able to sustain itself. It's so worth trying to achieve an open honest relationship. You will be able to make yourself happy. You won't have to worry before trying new things. You and your spouse can take risks together. You can discover each other and have the best experiences in life that you could wish for.

Chapter 12: Ten Steps to Happiness

1. Decide if it is worth forgiving. This step is the most important. Before recovering from the incident, you need to understand if it is important. No matter how much you love him/her, to forgive a betrayal is the most difficult challenge you can ever face. Here are some possible reasons to forgive. It happened only once. Maybe you fought, and he/she, after drinking a glass too many, ended up in bed with another person. Your partner is sorry for what happened, is depressed and would do anything to prove their repentance. If you think you have a really special relationship, it's better to resist the temptation to leave to see if you can recover it. You don't want to give up your relationship, especially if you've been with this person for a long time and your relationship is healthy and intimate. Discovering a betrayal, of course, will put all this in doubt. You should analyze the whole story before making a decision.

Don't ever forgive a serial traitor. If they have already done it and you have children and a life together, it's not worth it. Maybe it's the first time you have caught them, but they have betrayed you many times already. Do not forgive a betrayal if you are with this new person. It will be almost impossible to build a solid relationship on this foundation. If betrayal is a sign of a relationship destined to fail, do not try hard. Two people who have nothing in common, who do not feel very attracted to each other and who are unable to make the relationship work, have no future. To forgive takes a big heart. You may get reminded of the betrayal at certain moments which may make you leave them and never see them again. In those times, focus on what is tying you to the person. Count their remorse and urge them to make amends as part of your healing process and also reflect on your inner self. It is necessary that it's not just a compromise and that you feel happy. It is pointless to still be in the relationship and make the other person feel sorry all the time or expect them to be apologetic every step of the way.

2. Take the time to calm down after the initial chaos. You don't want to talk about it right away or argue about it. That could make things worse for you as well the unfaithful spouse. Take a walk, go to the gym or cry in your room. Distract yourself as much as possible. You may want to express your anger or do something that harms the person. On the contrary, you may even get inclined towards causing harm upon yourself. Be aligned to the emotions before thinking rationally. This process could take a few weeks, so you should move away from them. If you live together, stay at the home of a friend or family member or in a hotel. Take some time off and lose any kind of touch with them. Be ready to face them only after taking some time off to come in terms with the situation. You can be filled with doubts and questions at this point so creating a distraction rather than overthinking is preferred. Think about why this happened with you both and how could you have overlooked this happening all this while, can cloud your brain. You may feel a pressing need to talk to the person. But

it is much better to refrain from this to find some peace.

3. Don't blame yourself. Don't think your partner has betrayed you because you're not attractive or interesting or because of work or you let your children absorb you too much. The fault of the betrayal is of the person who betrays, there is no excuse unless you have betrayed them first. In that case, it's a different story. However, although it is not your fault, you may have done something to contribute to the degradation of the relationship. Every human being is allowed to make mistakes. But no excuse can be big enough to involve someone other than your partner in your life. The cheating partner can manipulate you by shifting the light on your mistakes. If a couple faces any problems and they can't deal with them appropriately, they should leave each other. There is always an option to leave your partner because you both aren't happy. If you are the single person who is unhappy with your partner, own up to your decision to leave them. Then search for someone else or pursue another dear relationship in your

life. If they provide an excuse for your shortcomings then that can be argued by saying if that were the case, the concerns should have been discussed openly. If the discussion doesn't go well or the other person still refuses to change, they can end the relationship and move on. Never let the traitor blame you. If that happens, cut the thread off without thinking twice. If you cheated on your partner first and you still stay together only to find out your partner is cheating on you, it's unfair. This is not acceptable and ideally you must move away from this person. If you as a couple couldn't get past the initial cheating, you should have not come together and tried to make it work. Time and emotions are precious. It is not exemplary to take revenge on the person by cheating on them to make them taste their own medicine.

4. Finance and financial pressures can ruin a relationship. There may be a change in circumstances such as you losing a job, you find out your assets are undervalued, their expenses are a lot higher than what they used to be. People have incurred additional costs as a couple they may get

involved in things that are costing them more money. These can create financial problems. Another problem can be that we have higher expectations and increasing needs. There is nothing wrong with wanting more but debt can be very easy to come by thorough big credit card bills or finance debts. They may start mounting up and before we know it the pressure becomes too much. Ironically, people increase their expenditure at times of being under pressure which really gets them stuck in a vicious cycle. If you are not feeling good and you are looking for ways to alleviate the pressure, you might book a trip or go out for a movie or restaurant which can make you spend more money worsening your situation. Another aspect is not knowing how to cope with the uncertainty of a person's reaction.

When you first enter a relationship, you don't have any financial burdens, but the pressure starts to build up eventually. What has changed? You have goals and things you want to achieve together. If you want to make a commitment to staying together, you want to build a life together. A big part of our lives is finance management. You want to buy a house or have a place to raise your children and develop a lifestyle. As more of these things come along, they all add to financial cost. Things tend to cost more than we expect them to. Things are going to invariably cost more because if you are buying a house you will also have to buy things to fill up the empty spaces. Raising children is very expensive. Specifically, men and women behave differently when facing financial pressures. Women facing this burden would like to talk it out. They express their feelings in words. If you are a man and a woman is describing her financial problems, the man needs to know that she is not looking for a solution necessarily. They tend to process their thoughts out loud. That's a completely opposite reaction to that of men. Men usually shut down when they are under financial pressures. Men have this attitude that it is their personal responsibility to solve all the problems in the marriage. They are biologically wired to achieve goals of a perfectly stable lifestyle. Go back to caveman days when the man's role was to go out and hunt for food. So, having financial problems can pose a problem to their masculinity because it hasn't been solved and it hits their self-esteem. This is an obvious generalization and may not hold true in every case in exactitude. But you can see some patterns of this behavior in your marriage. You should understand that they are just trying to deal with the problem as individuals and it has nothing to do with you. If you find out that financial pressures are affecting your marriage, be more aware of how you are addressing this issue. You may view your financial burden as something that you can individually deal with and not let that affect your marriage, you assume that you shouldn't bring your problems back home or you must share everything with your spouse maintaining the sanctity of marriage, it will be ideal. Acknowledge the problem. Don't brush it aside or pretend it doesn't exist. Don't try to suppress your awareness or focus. You need to start becoming financially educated. Start from setting financial goals. You can sit down with your spouse and plan out what you want to achieve.

Check how much you have and pay off any debts first. Set a date by when you want to pay off or collect a certain amount of saving. The next step is to reduce your expenses and increase your savings. See what you can cut out and what you don't particularly value. In this process, you will realize that you have started valuing money. Then you can aspire to increase your income. It can be achieved in so many ways today. You don't have to worry about getting a raise or picking more jobs. You can sell things on eBay and do a number of things online. You can easily find some fun new ways of increasing your income. The next step is to agree with your partner to share your goals and you both take responsibility to achieve the ultimate result. It's important for both the parties to not blame and actually engage in providing for each other's needs. They can also resolve so much by providing each other with support. If you are a woman you can get more involved and take initiative to inculcate financial values. You can give your husband an idea and input. Men must agree to share the responsibility so that this doesn't become the reason for the end of your relationship.

5. Make sure your partner is willing to recover the relationship. If you decide to forgive him, you will need to make sure that he wants to resume the journey with you, even if it takes months or years to start feeling good again. Make sure your partner is genuinely sorry. There is a beautiful difference between saying and being sorry. Make sure that, in addition to being sorry, he is willing to stay with you. A real sense of happiness can be achieved if you stop getting intimidated by the fear of the relationship ending or getting a divorce. The more you are scared of the break up the more it is likely to happen. If the thought of splitting up makes you anxious, angry or depressed then you probably have certain fears about it. This is not a judgment because fears are completely natural. But these fears can't help you. Common fears while people are trying to get a divorce are security or emotional fears. Security fears include if you get divorced where will you live? How will I earn money, raise children, make a good lifestyle? How will children

deal with divorce? Men may worry about their finances splitting and clever lawyers hired by their wives. Comprehend which of these fears apply to you. Emotional fears can be about how you will feel if you get a divorce. Some of these fears are what will society think of me- friends, colleagues, family? Will you be able to keep your friends? What if they outcast you and feel like they don't want anything to do with you again? Will your children still love you? Will you be able to provide the same upbringing which your spouse and you could have provided together? Are they going to turn out well adjusted? Will you ever find love again? Is it too painful to get a divorce? These are the questions to ask if you have any of these thoughts applying to your life. But if you really want to save your marriage you need to stop worrying about it coming to an end. Because the fear will keep your mind off the process of actually making that change. It's said that whatever you fear will come upon you. Fear makes you weak and when you are weak you are unattractive. Your spouse will be likely to leave you. If you worry all the time, and you are tearful angry or hurt, they won't enjoy being with you. Fear makes you reactive and not proactive. If you just react and you fall in the downward spiral of things, it will be very difficult to recover your marriage. This can drive you to do all the wrong things rather than the right things. It can stop you from dealing with the reality of your situation. You can either recover or get back your lost love or else your relationship can come to an end and you will never see the other person again. Only these two scenarios are likely to happen. One of these things is going to happen. It will be either soon or later. People tend to get complacent that everything will be fine along the way. But this situation never lasts forever. Because eventually one person will get sick of how things are or some better alternative comes along in their lives. You need to be prepared for both these situations. It is best to prepare for any situation that may come your way. Having overcome your fear will help you rise to the occasion much better. To get rid of your fears look at each of your fears clearly and see which of these are actually true. We sometimes imagine that something is going to happen, but it isn't the case. Ask yourself are you really penniless and homeless? Don't you have your close ones who love you enough to be there for you at this time of atrocity? It is not generally the case that there is no source of light at the end of the tunnel for you. Create a picture of a positive picture without any negativity from the spouse. Just include the positive points. This is not to encourage yourself to get divorced. It will make you positive and bring you in a much more attractive place in life. You will feel rejuvenated rather than sulking and feeling vulnerable.

6. You will both have to acknowledge your feelings and accept the pain and confusion that you will not miss. Tell them how you feel and make sure they know what is happening to you. Before you can recover the relationship, your partner will have to understand that they have put you in a terrible position. Of course, even they are not good, but make sure they understand you. Some people have real issues in their marriage. They have fallen out of love and the communication is gone, and the

sexual attraction is not there anymore. Of course, the biggest challenge is the affair itself. The most difficult situation is when one person really tries to save the marriage and the other really doesn't want to stay and just wants to leave. They lose sight of themselves. When a person is still holding on to the relationship and really trying to repair it to make the spouse happy, they feel all the problems will come to an end. Even though this is true, all of the people focus on pleasing their spouse and none of them think about comforting themselves. They are putting their own needs last and this is especially true in the case of women. They put their children and husband before them but in the process they themselves become miserable. This is doing you more harm than good. If you place another's needs before your own, you will end up unhappy which will increase your stress. You will feel depressed, your heath, productivity and work will suffer. It can also strain your other relationships. You may eventually begin to be resentful towards your spouse. You have been putting all this effort in and either you fail to get anything back or you simply are not getting the result you want. Being sad and unhappy makes you look unattractive to the other person. This will make you both unhappy and the relationship won't be able to sustain itself. The important thing to save here is your soul. Here soul is not being used in a religious sense at all. You have to keep intact and really save the essence of who you are. What does it look like to be really who you are? It begins with doing things that you really love to do. You spend your life and time in things that you enjoy doing. You are able to speak your mind off and say out loud everything you want without having the fear of being criticized. You are confident and you realize everyone's reaction to what you say or feel is really their own concern. You must do the things that make you happy. Learning to be and enjoy is really the most important thing to do.

7. Talk about what happened honestly. Don't rush into the conversation. It is not about arguing, but about discussing it rationally: Ask him what happened. He must not go into intimate details but tell you how many times he has seen the other

person and when. Ask him what he feels about the other person. Your partner might tell you that he doesn't want to share anything, but then you'll have to make sure of it. Ask him if it happened before you found out, so you'll know more before making a final decision. Knowing the past doesn't always help, but the damage is done now. Ask him what he thinks of your relationship. Find out why he cheated and what his intentions are. Repeat how you feel. At this point, you have already communicated your emotions widely, but maybe you have changed your mind after hearing the whole story. Discuss what to do to make the relationship work. You could take notes and figure out what mistakes to avoid for you to get stronger. Spend more time together, be honest or completely change your routine. You can go to a psychologist, talk about your problems with your friends or solve everything yourself. Set rules. If your partner cheated on you at work, do they have to change jobs? Many experts say yes. Does your partner have to call you often when he is out? This could be humiliating but remember that you have also received your dose of humiliation.

8. Work on having more open communication every day: Talk about your true feelings at least once a week. This step should not be forced, but do not underestimate it. Tell yourself how you feel. Talk about both positive and negative emotions, even if you have distanced yourself after the betrayal. Don't be passive-aggressive. If you are angry, say it when it's time. The problem people have when they start to see their marriage fail is they simply don't know what to do. You are currently faced with the prospect of ending your relationship for some reason. Probably the two of you have just drifted apart. It has taken time and you are not connecting the same way as you used to. There is no fulfillment or enjoyment left in the marriage. Have you tried counseling or therapy for your relationship? Are you discussing your problems with your spouse or trying to discuss them? Have you pleaded with them or threatened them? Have you done any nice things for them? Have you tried to make them feel guilty? Then see

if any of these actually worked. Have they had a positive impact? Has this brought you closer together or has it gone the opposite way and made things worse? If all these things don't work, then what does work? Understanding the answer to that comes down to one thing- you have to leave the need to save your marriage. You need to focus on yourself and really care about your present and future.

9. Work on improving the relationship. You will have to cultivate the relationship. Here's what to try: Devote yourself to an interest or a hobby together. Share more interests. If you have distanced yourself because you have nothing in common, choose something to bring you closer, like choosing a book each month that you will either read or watch a TV show together. It seems little, but you will notice the difference. Make compromises. In a relationship both should win. Go on vacation together. Doing something new will be a breath of fresh air. A journey is not a long-term solution, but it will give you time to reflect and to be alone together. Stop blaming your partner. It

may seem impossible, but if you want things to work between you, you won't have to blame their mistakes. Talk about it only when you tell them how you feel. Don't humiliate your partner or push them to make sure of your love over and over again: this is exhausting.

10. Do not be obsessed with the person with whom has betrayed you, or you will go crazy and ruin the relationship. If you know them and you go to the same social tours, avoid meeting them. Strive to forget their existence. Don't compare yourself to this person and feel inferior to their alleged qualities. Don't judge them if you don't know them. Maybe they fell in love with your partner or didn't know they were married. Don't follow them on Facebook or on other social networks trying to understand what they have that you don't have. Don't even follow them in real life. Don't talk about them with your partner. Focus on your relationship. If you are obsessed with this person and you can't help it, talk to a friend. Stop.

Chapter 13: Conclusions

When two people meet in a relationship with an element of passion that sustains and their union ends in marriage, they may not be aware of what is to follow. Sometimes they may have difficulty keeping everything together or reconciling. Love is messy and infidelity is even more disorderly. There is no way to get your heart through all the problems and come clean and become strong again together. To ensure normality it is necessary to have something to hold onto. Some infidelities resolve quickly, but some may have difficulty ending. This reluctance must be worked out. People who want to rebuild the relationship after being scammed are on a hard journey. At the time of being destroyed, you don't trust what they say. You lose confidence in others and in yourself. It is a loss of a partner and a loss of self. Try to find a purpose and never lose hope. If the person left you without giving you the answers you deserved, embrace them. Feel hurt and move on. A healthy and safe future awaits you.

Having a relationship without criticism, without resentment, without cheating is just a place where you two will be happy to be together and support each other. Each of us should really try to reach that place in our relationships where there is complete honesty and space to breathe. If you feel that being honest is difficult or workable for you, there are a few things you can do to significantly increase the amount of honesty and enjoy all the good things in your relationship. The first is to be honest with yourself and to yourself. The relationship you have with others is a reflection of yours with you. If you want something in life and you think you can't tell your spouse maybe because they may not approve, then move that thought away, just ask yourself what you really want here. Imagine it theoretically and it becomes really clear. So, imagine t the worst thing that can happen if you tell your partner what you're hiding. You may think they will get angry. Maybe they will or not. But if they get angry, they will have to deal with it and the chances are they will get over it. But getting angry is something that can be addressed. So, you have to understand what is the best thing that could happen. You can actually get what you want and share happiness with your partner. An example of this is when a husband in therapy revealed that he wanted to go to a nudist beach and go scuba diving and sunbathe had. He felt embarrassed to say it out loud because he feared his wife would judge him. So, it is really necessary to prove total honesty. The next step is to create an environment of trust. You decide to never make your spouse feel bad about what they say or do. Don't judge them for their thoughts and feelings. Allow them to make mistakes. The last step is to guarantee total honesty from this point onwards.

I wish you the best of luck and I hope this has helped your soul to heal and your relationship has become stronger.

Thank you for purchasing this book and I hope that reading it was an interesting and educational experience. I put all my efforts, enthusiasm and heart into every sentence I wrote. The main objective of this book is to help, with my experience, my readers to understand and overcome betrayal which is a profound and devastating malaise. If you liked it and above all it influenced your life and helped you along the way, I ask you for five minutes of your time to write down what you think of the book by leaving a review, because it would help other people improve their lives. The opinions of my readers I always treasure for my work and it would help me improve my way of communicating and give me new ideas to develop.

I mentioned my email for advice, criticism and suggestions. You will also receive a notification of the publication of my other works.

Thanks,

Suellen McDolly

Email ID: qr.publishinghouse@gmail.com

Printed by Amazon Italia Logistica S.r.l.
Torrazza Piemonte (TO), Italy

10278930R00093